To my dog, Chiquisonte, who is constantly making me vibrate in the most beautiful frequency in which a human being could possibly be, love.

HOW I WON THE LOTTERY WITH THE LAW OF ATTRACTION

Acknowledgements

I would like to express my deepest gratitude to Dr. Joseph Murphy, whose literary works helped me to change my way of thinking and made me understand that I was in this world to achieve everything I wanted and be happy.

I would also like to thank all those who weekly upload content to their YouTube channels and help people like me to awaken their consciousnesses.

Finally, I want to thank my girlfriend and my friend Rulo for standing by my side in the most difficult times and helping me to continue evolving.

INDEX

Structure

This book is divided into three uneven parts. In the first one, I'll tell you my personal story in relation to lottery manifestation. I'll start with a brief introduction about some basic aspects of the Law of Attraction. Then, I'll develop its operation in my life, first unconsciously and then by putting every single tool this Law gives us to work with the purpose of realizing my dream of winning the Argentinian Lottery.

The second part is the shortest (it's not the least important, though). This section aims for the readers to self-analyze themselves. It consists of a series of questions that have the power to help you manifest, no matter where you are or your way of life.

In the third and last segment I'll explain to you, with my very own personal touch and based on my life experience, some manifestation techniques. These mechanisms helped me manifest the lottery and still help me today, to obtain the best results in every single objective I have in mind. They became part of my daily routine, a way of living and feeling.

As you can see, each part is different as regards the way I had to approach them, but the goal in every case is that you connect with your own emotions and dreams in a positive way. I have no doubt that it is going to be the case.

I want to inspire you to accomplish every single goal you have in your life with my own personal experience. In my case, it was money by winning the lottery, but it can be whatever you want: better health, relationships, or freedom in general. My adventure gave me a series of learnings and I'm going to pass them on to you to absorb them and benefit from them in your own life.

I'm a 'normal' person. I don't have a university degree and I'm not a famous sportsperson. Before the BIG day, I had been working in my father's business for three years, I couldn't make extra money for my family and my self-esteem was painfully low. I was in a situation that many of you can relate with at this moment, and I want you to know that if you are willing to make some positive changes, everything you aspire to manifest in your life is possible.

In my case, I needed a change. I wasn't happy with my life. The Law of Attraction caught my attention so much that I became a regular reader of contemporary spirituality at first, and later on I started to incorporate other topics, such as personal development, finance and even psychology. With this, I want to show that you can fulfill your dreams too, and this universal law is an excellent starting point, an ally.

I want you to answer the questions, so you can identify clearly what you wish and find out the perfect way to manifest it. Many of you may believe that you know what kind of life you would like to have, but if you open up and self-analyze, the chances are most of you won't be able to explain the basics of that "ideal of life". Taking the time to answer them will train your mind and activate emotions that will help you to achieve your goals.

Last but not least, I transcribed well-known techniques for those Law of Attraction practitioners, but with my very own personal touch, using my experiences with my manifested wish as a reference. I have also dared to write some personal advice, as it was fundamental in my journey to winning the lottery and it still is today, helping me to be A HAPPY PERSON!

Preface

This book is a story narrated in first person. Here I will tell you all about the process that I walked through to finally manifest the jackpot in my country's lottery, all thanks to the conscious use of the Law of Attraction.

I decided to write this anonymously, as Argentina's current economic situation and lack of security doesn't allow me to reveal my name and maintain my current life. And as you may understand, the last thing I do is have that horrendous feeling even in my house.

I am Argentine, I am younger than 40 years old and I would like to give you all a bit of the information that I had to acquire in my journey to the manifestation of my wish. Mood changes is something that I had to bear with in my daily life, and it's possible that you suffer that inside revolution too. And don't panic: it's something that every single person that is expecting to win the lottery using LOA may suffer. I would like my own experience to help all the readers, so as not to make the same mistakes I made.

I am going to show you with real-life situations of my own, how I changed my way of thinking with regards to money, love and health, so as to be ready for the big moment, the moment of manifesting my ultimate dream.

I understood the importance of money, the happiness you can generate by administering and using it correctly. I learned about mental blocks related to being rich that we combat from an early age, transforming them progressively so as to open the door wide to economic abundance.

Another aspect I'm going to focus on is how we should prioritize respecting and valuing ourselves before committing to a relationship with another person. What would you say if I state 'nothing is more toxic in a couple than unconditional love from one or both sides'?

We human beings underestimate our health because we tend not to care about it until the moment something happens and only there we acknowledge its remarkable importance.

My thought and action balance in health, love and money allowed me to align with the desire of becoming a millionaire by winning the lottery. Have you thought about what you really want in your life? Do you have an action plan? Do you believe you can make it? I assure you, no matter what your wish is, that if you let your emotions guide you, the Universe, God or whatever you believe in will open the correct path for you to manifest it.

'THE VIBRATION
IN WHICH YOU
WANT TO BE
EXISTS, BUT
IT IS YOUR
JOB TO ALIGN
YOURSELF'

FIRST PART

<u>Sorry and thank you</u>

First of all, I would like to say that I'm sorry for the informality of my writing. It is probable that you'll find mistakes or things could have been written better. I am not a professional author; in fact, I couldn't be farther from that. However, I believe that I can write my experience down in order to make someone realize that they can use it for their own purposes.

On another note, LET ME TELL YOU, I'm not selling a magic formula to win money in any kind of game of chance, or even the lottery. You're about to read a story, the story of my evolution, that among numerous effects, manifesting a huge amount of money in the lottery was one of them.

There were several objectives that made me write this book: one of them is that, when you finish it, you'll be able to incorporate in your life new knowledge about my experience that will help you face life easily. In this way, you'll be in an excellent position to obtain what you want. I want to help you achieve or regain your ambition, that ambition that you need to attain your goals. Everything depends on you. We need to analyze our emotions as human beings, as Esther and Jerry Hicks say, 'understanding that we are in the first line of thought', but above all, leaving excuses and faults aside. You shouldn't blame others for your incapability of having the life you desire. Your happiness depends on someone, and you are that someone.

I thank you because every minute you devote to this book is precious for you. And you, among an ocean of books, chose my work. I am going to inspire you so that you can live most of your life in your peak state. No matter your current state of mind, you'll be able to crest.

Most of us were made to believe that our aspirations mustn't be pretentious because of different reasons, but I assure you they are wrong. How can that be done? The best starting point is to change little by little your way of thinking, getting closer to your spiritual side, until you clear away your doubts and understand the basic idea that, naturally, you have your own right to feel well in every sense of your life.

As you change your way of thinking, you'll see that your life will adjust to your ideals accordingly. This job doesn't have an estimated timeframe, but it does have a huge reward. And that reward can be, if you desire it, the lottery jackpot.

Always based on my personal experience, I will convey my own learning in the way to being successful manifesting the lottery. How I let go my wish of winning millions in the lottery, only to see it realized later. I learned that the moment we commit ourselves with what we long for, the Universe or God will give us the strength we need to achieve our dreams.

One of my main motivations, the one that made me start writing, is to help all those who are interested in manifesting the lottery. I know this group is particularly substantial, and I also know that this wish can generate great hopes. I would love every single reader to experience the heavenly situation of winning the lottery, and I don't say it won't be possible. I want you to obtain knowledge from this book, regardless of your success with money. I made a lot of mistakes that made me feel shattered (from panic attacks to depression) and I would like nobody else to suffer what I suffered.

You may think, as I would do, that you have the situation under control, or that those problems won't be part of your life. But when you build your hopes up and you don't get what you were expecting, the situation may get you out of control and affect you in a lot of unexpected ways.

I had nobody to check this book for me. I decided to do it in a spontaneous way, because I want to reach you in my full genuineness. I am going to share with you in the clearest possible way the phase of my life in which I started to feel that I could win the lottery using the LoA, until the moment this book is finished, time after the big day.

I am going to tell you in the most detailed way the how and why I think I was successful. How I got into the correct vibrational frequency that this manifestation requires, and if you are one of those that needs to know everything, I am going to go into specific details about the big day and the winning numbers, I remember every single thing I did that day. What was the first thing I bought? Was I able to maintain my wealth, or did I waste it?

Another reason that made me write this book is that a considerable number of authors agree in saying that nobody should aspire to be successful with the lottery. They say that "probabilities are one in more than one million", "it's better to make money by working hard" or "more likely to be struck by lightning than win the lottery". I am going to explain to you why all those people are wrong.

I used to read stories of jackpot winners that eventually end up in somber situations, and that's another reason why I decided to tell my story to the world. This story is different, because not only did it have a happy ending, but also was achieved by the conscious use of the LoA.

Instead of getting carried away by probability analysis as many lottery players do, I decided to follow my emotions and my aspirations. By doing that, I managed to win an amount of money that allowed me to achieve many of my dreams, dreams that long before they were only in my imagination.

The path to success brought a lot of change to my life, but each alteration was important and necessary to align myself with what I was hoping. Thus, I'm going to describe them in detail. After all, they were preparing me to perfectly manifest my wish.

You are going to read my story, yes, but while you do it, I have no doubts you'll activate emotions that will play a part in the achievement of your goals. What will you do in case you are able to manifest the lottery? If it exists in your mind, it can happen.

"Miracles exist, and they can happen to you"

Deepak Chopra

Law of Attraction

"The vast majority of people are born, grow up, struggle and go through life in misery and failure, not realizing that it would be just as easy to switch over and get exactly what they want out of life, not recognizing that the mind attracts the thing it dwells upon."

Napoleon Hill

I assume that if you were drawn to this book, it means that you have some basic knowledge regarding the wonderful Law of Attraction (LoA). In my case, I reached success with a very specific and important wish: how to manifest and win millions at the lottery. I don't consider myself an expert, on the contrary, I am constantly trying to keep learning to continue to reap the benefits of this law on a daily basis. I know this is a topic with a lot of ground to cover, but what I set myself to do here is to explain how the LoA functions in a short and easy to understand way.

This universal law is rooted in the idea that through the emotions we put out (thoughts and feelings) we can attract positive and negative things into our lives. Everything is energy. The type of energy you emit comes back to you.

Family, friends, mentors, teachers, books, videos and even newspapers or magazine articles can help you in teaching you how to use the LoA. It's important to clarify that, like with any other law, the practical aspect differs from the theorical one. The ultimate objective of all of us who seek to consciously benefit from this law is to obtain happiness, and while it doesn't work in the same way for everyone, the reality is that IT ALWAYS WORKS for everybody, be it consciously or unconsciously.

One of the most common reasons as to why the LoA doesn't seem to work for a lot of people, is that they are unaware as to how to apply it to themselves with success. They don't know what the most effective way to benefit from it is. This is because we usually attract into our lives what our emotions feel at the present time, with the help of our own steady and constant actions. If you focus on the absence of your wish more than in its manifestation, there's a possibility that what this law processes in your brain is the "no", the absence. Often this occurs because people lack faith, they can't feel their desire as real before it physically manifests. The opposite also happens, with people not respecting the timing of the manifestation and getting in the way of it. But I don't want to get ahead of myself, I'll expand on this topic further down the line.

> *"Faith enables the believing soul to treat the future as present and the invisible as seen"*
>
> *Dr. J Oswald Sanders*

In some cases, we can manifest our desires in a

quick and easy way, but sometimes it takes effort and constancy. This is because you might have obtained good results in the short term but, to be successful in life with this law, it is of utmost importance to know how to interpret different variables, like knowing when to persist and when to let go.

To be able to manifest winning the lottery I had to change my then-way of thinking, beliefs and feelings and actions.

When I started getting interested in the LoA, I quickly stumbled upon the books of two of the greatest masters it has, Esther and Jerry Hicks. If you haven't yet read them, I suggest you do so. They explain with clarity and certainty how to manifest our desires with the conscientious use of the LoA.

If you want to manifest something important that can change your life (like I did), you will find that the path you'll walk is going to be riddled with a plethora of challenges and it'll be up to you to take advantage and make the best out of the situation. This will prepare you to be ready to receive your wish.

I'm going to bring forth my example of how the LoA works, using the steps taught by Esther and Jerry Hicks. Please have in mind that by following these steps anyone can obtain benefits in any aspect they desire in their lives, be it love, money or health.

The lottery manifestation is very complicated and almost impossible to achieve for the majority of people, but thanks to my experience I can ascertain that once you understand and follow the steps properly, that the Universe, God or the life force will grant you what you yearn for.

Not being aligned with what we long for can make the manifestation of winning the lottery take longer or not to happen. In a materialistic world where economics are of great importance, suddenly acquiring too much money signifies a big change in the life of anyone. To make this big vibrational jump, it's possible that we have to sort through all types of changes.

Before I explain my experience with "The Hicks Theory", I want to go over another fundamental aspect: the power of intention.

Everything starts with a thought. When you set a goal, you must know that it will be achieved through action. Without action there's no LoA. That strength, that movement is what propels you forward to find results. If you don't act, no amount of sitting around at home while you visualize your desire or do any type of manifestation exercise (which I'll explain in the third part) will work.

If you want to win the lottery, at the very least, you have to go to an agency and buy a ticket. You can't wait around hoping someone gives you one or to magically find one laying on the street and expect it to be the winning one. This is the first necessary action that you must do. The most important task afterwards will be to work daily on elevating your vibrational frequency until you are aligned with what you want to attract (in my case it was the lottery jackpot).

Activating the power of intention is a process in which your discipline, wisdom, love and selflessness are connected, and its purpose is to put you in touch with your natural being, leaving aside the absolute power that our ego usually has over us. This power can push us towards our dreams becoming a reality, but throughout our journey we have to adopt changes in regard to our new way of seeing life.

Theory of the Masters

> *You are the creator of your own experience ... whether you know it or not. Your life experience unfolds as an exact response to your thoughts ... whether you know it or not". Esther y Jerry Hicks*

According to the theory of Esther and Jerry Hicks, to manifest a desire three steps are required...

1- **Ask**: This step is the simplest and we do it in a natural way. You don't have to use words, just by feeling you are already putting out there into the world what you desire as a petition.

This step is completely up to you. What do you

want? I asked to win the lottery. It appears to be something anyone yearns for, and I don't blame them because when you achieve it, life gets so much easier and happier in almost every aspect. But this doesn't mean you have to ask for a ton of money from one moment to another. You can wish for anything, love, a job, to improve your health, there are no limits.

Once I decided to manifest millions by winning the lottery, unknowingly, I started the difficult path of aligning myself with that frequency. That desire brought forth a lot of changes and if one isn't prepared or is unable to interpret that these changes occur to help us grow and evolve, then they will considerably worsen a lot of aspects from our life. The manifestation might stall midway, and in the case that it even goes through, you might end up feeling unhappy and dissatisfied.

2-   **Get answers**: This step has NOTHING to do with the physical aspect. Every request is handled, be it a trip, a cup of coffee or winning the lottery. In the beginning I implored for my wish with prayers and emotions. The problem was that I was vibrating at a completely different frequency, which is why my desire didn't manifest and I assume this is the reason why 99% of people who play the lottery don't succeed.

My way of thinking didn't align with my desire of what it meant to become a millionaire in a day.

Months before winning the lottery, I was already a happy, grateful person, but it was then that I started receiving very specific signals that would become a part of my life. I'll detail them throughout the book.

During the manifestation process of my wish, the apparition of signals became a frequent occurrence, which in my mind meant that something great was going to happen. During my darkest times they kept me going. If I wanted to succeed, giving up was not an option.

These signs generated emotions that were in tune with my wish. I'd seen videos about these types of situations on several occasions, but I paid them no mind until these signals started to awaken feelings of joy and exhilaration inside of me. They were signals...

Months before winning the lottery, I would see with an impressive frequency the repetition of some numbers, for example: 333-111-1111-999. I can't explain why this situation brought me so much happiness, but it was as if some kind of energy was helping me stay positive and to keep believing. These positive emotions helped me go through my daily activities.

Another circumstance that suddenly became a regular thing in my life was a van from the lottery agency parked every morning on the entrance of the apartment building where I used to live. Maybe an employee from the lottery agency lived in the same building and the van was just there to pick him up, I don't know, but what I do know is that every time I went out to go to work, I would see the van and it made me very happy.

Another signal that I want to emphasize is that all of a sudden, I started to see the car that I said I would buy if I won the lottery. I was on a really high frequency in comparison with prior months. I understand that this situation is connected to the fact that I included the car in my daily thoughts because it was part of my visualizations and I felt like it was already mine, despite knowing that it wasn't a possibility to buy it. Nevertheless, this sign made me cheerful.

Lastly, I would like to remark on dreams. Even though many people think that they don't have any importance, I believe the opposite. Having a good dream gives us happy and positive emotions when we wake up, which makes getting up in a good mood a reality. This is why I believe that they can be indicators that let us know that we are moving in the right direction.

In the process in which I set myself on to win the lottery with the help of LoA, I used to dream that I found coins, that in my bedroom drawer there was a lot of cash, trips, winning the lottery and more happy things. None of these dreams were recurring but the themes were similar in the way that, in all of them, me and my loved ones were happy.

These situations showed me that I was on the right path, moving towards the place I had chosen, and able to reach anywhere I wanted fueled by my faith.

You can choose whether to believe or not, I chose to believe that all these occurrences were sent to give me strength by means of the positive emotions that emerged in me when I saw the signs. "Good vibes" as they are commonly called nowadays. I channeled these signals towards my happiness and well-being.

3-   **Let it flow towards you**: This step also depends solely on you and it's the last one you need to execute to see the manifestation of your desire. It's about the art of allowing. It's when you adapt your life in lieu of what you wish for, it's the alignment of your vibrational frequency with the thing you asked for.

This book is mainly about what this step was like for me, but at the start, it wasn't an easy task to understand what this phase was about.

Going by the theory I knew that I needed to align my vibrational frequency with what my wish required, but I never thought that for this to happen, my life would be turned upside down (with every change having the goal of my wish being granted).

The first thing I had trouble with was with "letting

go", this part isn't easy at all. As human beings it's in our nature to get attached to all sorts of things, like people, objects, situations and in my case, my wish.

Most of us were raised under the idea that the only way to reach success is by working hard and winning the lottery would be something that totally contradicted this idea. Achieving that dream would mean becoming a millionaire in the blink of an eye, without any effort. But this simply wasn't true (not in the way I was seeking to succeed). The alignment to allow my desire to flow towards me, in a way that I could enjoy the arrival of my wish without letting it harm me, was something I had to work day in and day out.

As a result of my profound interest in the Law of Attraction, it took me no time to realize that I was making a terrible mistake by paying more attention to the ABSENCE of what I desired over WHAT I DESIRED. I wanted to manage the timing of its arrival without allowing it to flow towards me, which awakened contradictory emotions regarding the manifestation of my request.

I had to find a way for my thoughts and actions to coincide with what I was trying to attract. My request was clear, I knew that the Universe was backing me, and below, you will read the story of how I managed to align myself with the vibrational frequency of my wish, letting it flow towards me...

"There is no limit to what this law can do for you; dare to believe in your own ideal; think of the ideal as an already accomplished fact." Charles Haanel

The Law of Attraction works

We are a magnet, we attract what we feel...

While it's true that the concept of LoA isn't something new, its use is on the rise exponentially thanks to the testimony of well-known or famous people that claim to find success with it. But what happens to the rest of us?

The people we see living a "dreamy" lifestyle are regular practitioners of the Law of Attraction. In most cases they practice it in an intuitive way since it's highly possible that almost none of them have even read a single paragraph about this law. I could name you examples of athletes, artists, or successful politicians who practice the LoA, but as those aren't personal experiences that I can reliably prove, I would rather give you some personal examples, different from the one (winning the lottery) that gave birth to this book.

I want this example to help you clarify that we don't decide whether to use this law or not. It simply works.

"Everything that's coming into your life you are attracting into your life. And it's attracted to you by virtue of the images you're holding in your mind."

When I was 19 years old, I had taken a part time job at a salon where birthday parties of kids ages 3-9 take place. A few years prior to this, I was the youngest of 4 brothers until a new family member came into this world. After being together for several years my father and his new partner decided to have a child, and that's how the new addition came into our lives. This arrival was an uncommon event and an experience like nothing before in regard to kids. At that time, I didn't sympathize much with the little ones because being the youngest family member meant that I spent more time in the company of adults. This would all change thanks to the mighty LoA.

As I was saying, with this new family addition and my recent job, my contact with little kids went from being close to non-existent, to something regular. As an employee I was mostly in the administrative sector where I interacted with the parents rather than the children and even though I spent several hours a day with them, my relationship with the little ones was fleeting (I only saw them play, yell and that was it). I rarely had a child come up to me to ask or tell me something thinking I was one of the people animating the party. I had very little sympathy and patience for them.

One afternoon, one of the party entertainers didn't show up, and because he didn't phone in time, we couldn't find a replacement. My boss asked me if

I could fill in as a replacement and help with the games and some other aspects, which meant I had to interact with kids ages 3-4 at the party for over 3 hours.

During the day, one of the children managed to bring out significant emotions from me. During the birthday party the kid looked for me all the time to play. We talked and clicked in, and this completely changed the way children usually made me feel. When the celebration was over and the coordinators came to thank me for my help and to ask me about my thoughts regarding the experience, I answered with a phrase that will forever be engraved in my mind: "I felt splendid, I think I want to become a father right this second".

When I came back to my home, I made the same remark to my family. Whenever I got together with my friends at the club and saw little kids playing around, I came up to them to interact because I found it gratifying. From one second to the next, kids started to be a pleasant presence that filled me with positive emotions. I started offering help to take care of my baby sister on any occasion it was necessary and the emotions that I felt during that time were very strong and rewarding. I preferred that activity over going out with friends or doing the things 19 years old usually did.

A little over a year later, at just 20 years old, life gifted me with a beautiful daughter. In an unconscious manner my heartfelt words and the strong emotions I had experienced, kicked into motion the LoA. First, I asked for it with my words, then I added sensations and strong emotions, I got answers and I let it flow towards me.

Going back to the formula of the masters Esther and Jerry Hicks:

1- Ask

2- Get answers

3- Let it flow towards you

This example clearly shows that the Law of Attraction always works, any time and for everyone. There's not a single unique way to use its power, one can also be successful using tools that facilitate the arrival of what we desire, as was my experience with the lottery. But in this last case that I just told you about, I didn't know anything about the LoA, I wasn't aware of its existence but even then, in an unconscious way, I put it to work perfectly. That's how my daughter came into my life, changing it forever.

I only realized that this situation was created by me, long after I became a father. In fact, nowadays when I think about it, I keep being in awe at the power of this magnificent force known as the LoA. It's up to one to find the way to benefit from this law on a daily basis. There are no exceptions, if you take the time to think about the most important situations of your life, you'll realize that you were always the one responsible for them and that in some way, you allowed both good and bad into your life. The LoA was the protagonist in all these circumstances because all of them were a result of your thoughts, your intentions and actions.

I invite you to remember. Think about those important situations that you believe changed the course of your life and use those memories as a way to help you understand that you don't live randomly, that you are in fact, the true creator of your reality. Once it's clear (because it will), take full accountability and take the reins of your life forever, no more excuses. Forget about the guilt and the self-punishments, the universal laws are real, they exist and they are there to help us accomplish everything we put our minds into and to be happy.

If you think that there are situations that are hard to surpass, look back to the mistakes of the past without a heavy heart, resentment. Look at them like a gift to evolve because each and every single one surely left you with a valuable lesson. IF YOU ARE HERE, IT'S BECAUSE YOU HAVE THE RIGHT TO LIVE, TO BE HAPPY.

First conscious success

Use your thoughts to be in the same tuning as your desires: that is the first success you'll have with the conscious use of the Law of Attraction.

Thanks to the documentary "The Secret", I developed a big curiosity for the aspects of the Law of Attraction. I remember seeing it for the first time with my friends, and because of how intriguing I found it, I later paid more attention watching it by myself. From then on, I started watching YouTube videos, I bought books, I chatted with friends about the topic even though most of them found it ridiculous. This didn't affect me, and I kept getting more and more immersed in learning about this law.

At this stage I learned to meditate, visualize and to try getting up and going to sleep in a good mood, filled with positive thoughts. In some ways my life slowed down, I analyzed things more and I found happiness daily by feeling grateful for the little things in life.

During these first steps as a conscientious practitioner of this law I had some successful experience by combining visualizations and emotions. In just a few months I managed to make a trip that at one point seemed financially impossible for me during those days. But finally, the Universe opened doors for me that made it possible for me to make the trip.

If you ask me why I think that I was successful with that petition, the answer I give is always going to be the same: I asked, got an answer, let it go and received. This time (almost without meaning to) I implemented the correct step in an excellent manner. The reason why I could execute without any hassle the step that was (and is) the most difficult to me was by accident. I was just starting a relationship with my girlfriend so not being able to make the trip didn't seem so bad. Going away for a month without her didn't make all that happy. But the truth is that with the visualizations, meditations and the strong emotions I included in all my practices I had asked for my wish and the Universe answered me back by sending the economic means for me to achieve it.

The Universe started to show me that the LoA was serious, and the trip left me another valuable lesson that gave birth to a strong wish of becoming a millionaire. The lottery would be used as the medium and I would be using the LoA in a conscientious manner.

What I desired was to go to a very important sport event far away from my country. The price of the flight and show tickets, accommodation, food, etc. seemed to be way out of reach from me. Even more if we consider that the event was just 50 days away from the start and I didn't have a single dollar saved up.

As I was telling you, I had just recently started reading about the LoA and I decided to use that opportunity to put it to the test. Every night when I went to sleep, I thought that I was at the stadium rooting for my team or I pictured myself walking down the streets of a faraway country alongside my friends. When I meditated something similar used to happen, the emotions were so strong it was akin to actually experiencing those situations and the sensations were real and pleasant, to the point that after finishing my meditation the feeling of joy continued to flow through my body. I felt extreme happiness because the meditation experience orientated towards visualizing myself in the place that I wanted to be in the near future was absolutely real.

With only 30 days left for the start of the show and 0 dollars in my bank account, I started getting some clues that made me optimistic about my trip becoming a reality.

The first thing was the plane tickets. Out of curiosity, I checked the price of flights on the different sites that usually run promos and discounts. As the show was extremely popular worldwide and with so little time left for it to begin, I knew that it would be hard for an affordable fare. One afternoon, while I was drinking mate with my father at work, I checked the site and found a flight for the perfect date for an amazing price. When I told my dad about it, he commented that work had been going well for him the last couple of months and that while he could afford buying the plane ticket, he couldn't help me with the rest.

Despite the important step forward regarding my possibility of making the trip, I took it only as a signal, because I didn't have enough money to travel. I chose to be grateful for what happened, but I decided not to buy the plane ticket until I had more money.

I didn't want to make a rash decision by buying the first affordable ticket I had found, I needed to wait for more signals. I acted in the perfect way for the fulfillment of my wish to take place. I could have thought that if I didn't buy the ticket that I would never again get another opportunity and that way of acting would have been a disservice. Thankfully, at no point did anxiety get a hold of me.

It made me extremely happy that the Universe had sent me a concrete sign which meant I was doing things right. First by finding a plane ticket at a good price and later by giving me the means to buy it without having to drown in debt.

One night, while having dinner with friends, one of them commented that he had already paid for the whole trip, but he wasn't going to be able to make it. It turns out that in a few months his wife was going to go into labor with their first child and he didn't want to leave her alone. He didn't have this situation in mind when he bought the plane tickets, booked the hotels, transfers, tickets, etc. My friend along with some other people had organized this trip in advance and they had gotten excellent prices in everything I listed above, and if someone didn't take his place, he was going to lose the totality of his money.

The opportunity to make the trip came up less than a month from the start of the event and with the added bonus of having the prices be the ones from a year prior. I talked to my friend and told him that if he agreed, I could pay his part of the accommodations and event tickets in just a few months, but that the plane tickets were out of the question because they couldn't be transferred from one person to another. He thought it was a fantastic idea because either way, he would lose all the money he had already paid. The next step was verifying that the price of the plane tickets was the same as the day before so my father could afford to buy it. I admit that, while the dominant feeling in me at that time was joy, as I went towards the patio of the house I was in, I felt a little fearful of opening the app in my cellphone to check on the price of the plane tickets. Luckily, not only did I find the same tickets that I had previously seen but I also found them cheaper.

Everything started to align for the fulfillment of my wish. That same night I found myself having plane tickets, transfers, and the tickets for the event. The only thing missing was the money for the food expenses and other things that could come up during the trip. Less than a month away I didn't have time to save much until something unexpected happened.

Over a year before, I had been the victim of a car crash in which a vehicle crashed into mine from behind. As the insurance of this person that had hit me was taking too long with their paperwork to give me the check, I needed to get my car fixed, I ended up paying out of my own pocket. That insurance company had a bad reputation and I didn't want to wait for them to solve the problem of fixing my car. It would be too taxing, and I didn't want to go around with my car in that state, so I paid for the repairs myself while the paperwork was in progress.

Three days after I bought the plane tickets, I got a call from the insurance company asking me to go pick the check in my name. When I went to pick it up, I noticed that the face value gave me the possibility of paying off my friend and having some cash left to enjoy the trip. I didn't expect to cash in that money at that time because acquaintances who worked in that business had told me about how that particular company usually took years to pay.

I finally made the trip and as I previously mentioned I did it in an *almost* perfect way. This is because despite being profoundly grateful about being given the chance of doing it, being short on cash meant having too many limitations. These restrictions gave way to my strong desire to become a millionaire.

I became attentive to the actions people with a lot of money made. These actions were not something I often saw happening in my country. I started thinking that they were happier, they went about certain situations in such a natural way... situations that for the majority of people from my country would be almost impossible to do. For example: While I was sleeping at hostels along with 10 other individuals, they slept in any of the hundreds of hotels scattered around the city. I'm not even talking about the super luxurious ones; my friends and I couldn't dream of affording even the cheapest. Food? We ate at the hostel, in parks and squares.

These types of circumstances led me to think that if other people could live a more comfortable life, then so could I. After all, what was the difference between us? These types of thoughts and questions led me to feel curiosity in what being a millionaire was really like. I started watching videos, reading books as well as finance magazines and little by little I started changing the thought patterns I had grown up with. I had discovered that the biggest difference between first world and third world people was their mentality.

With all this information, along with my rising knowledge regarding the LoA, I thought that, If I had been able to achieve what once seemed impossible (the trip) then I could also achieve success with another wish.

What I didn't have in mind was that the mental unblocking to enjoy a good economic and financial situation was something completely different. It's a way of living, of thinking. If you want to win a sum of money that allows you to live comfortably for the rest of your life you need to change your mentality. When you hear about people who won the lottery and shortly after, not only lost everything but also ended up worse than when they started, it's because they weren't mentally prepared to face the situation. Almost any well-prepared person (with very rare exceptions) that hits the jackpot from one day to another is going to make that money multiply.

Coming back from that trip changed my life. Not only had I had my first success with the conscious use of the LoA, but my need to be a millionaire was born too.

Next, you will see how any supposed "failure" was one more step towards the manifestation of winning millions by playing the lottery. But first, I need you all to understand that the LoA isn't MAGIC. There are very specific mechanisms that can bring into your life anything you desire, but only if you take the time to understand them and put them into function. The mental blocks regarding money (especially for those of us who were born in Latin America) are something different, and it's up to you to work on changing this mindset. Read a lot, be well informed and use part of your free time to further educate yourself to create abundance and to eliminate excuses. For this, I recommend reading Jurgen Klaric, an author that gives very valuable information.

About the Law of Attraction, my first advice would be for you to be specific, feel as if you already have what you desire in your grasp, have faith and wait to receive it. Effort isn't always working hard, sometimes it just means aligning ourselves with what we want to manifest. It takes constancy, but if you really want it, then it might not be all that hard. Depending on your wish, you might change in a lot of aspects, but all of that will be a part of the process of your desire getting ready for you to receive it in the most perfect of ways.

"The Law of Attractions works in the same way the Law of Gravity works, neither one is precise, but they are both laws. Why do some people not want to agree? And why are some people so angry?

As soon as they admit that the Law of Attraction works, soon after, they have to assume the full responsibility of what they are receiving into their lives.

Few can admit it. It's a little scary. That means there's no one to blame. Think about the burden that it imposes on a person. If I could avoid responsibility,

I would too!

But once you understand the truth, there's no turning back"

Joe Vitale

Abundance: Plenitude and wellness

There are three fundamental pillars in which any person would wish to be successful so as to be able to lead a full and happy life: HEALTH, LOVE AND MONEY.

If one of these aspects isn't doing well, there's a high possibility that the other ones are thrown off balance. ABUNDANCE is a word I love and that encapsulates having all three aspects. When you are abundant, you are at every facet of your life, which means that you are healthy, you love and feel loved back, and that you have enough money to live your dream lifestyle.

It seems so easy to say it, but...how to achieve it? Or, in this case, how did I manage to enjoy living a life of prosperity and abundance.

The first thing I have to tell you is that there's obviously not a magical recipe for success, although I did learn a very effective one that worked for me and that I plan to share with you. It all depends on you, on knowing how to decode the emotions we as humans have; understanding that we are in the first line of thought for the creation of our own reality. Above all, you have to stop blaming other people and leave the excuses aside as to why you aren't leading the happy life you desire.

We all have inside the power to change the conditions in our lives to reach a state of abundance. The first step is recognizing that you are the one responsible for your present. Your thoughts and actions were the ones that put you in the place you are in now, be it good or bad. This is why there is no better way to face the rest of your life than accepting that you put yourself in that situation, and as a consequence, you'll be the protagonist of what will happen to you until the day you die (on your physical body).

Being abundant also means to be happy with what you are. While it's true that no one can be happy 24/7, those of us who have a mindset of abundance maintain a certain way of thinking that grants us emotional stability, which is a part of what makes us happy as individuals.

I always saw the lottery as a way to become a millionaire, but I had never imagined that trying to manifest it (using the LoA) would give me so many lessons that would end up making me a better person in every single way.

While I had moments where I was happy before being a millionaire, I wasn't anywhere close to being abundant and prosperous, I was still vastly short on money. I was super healthy, had a family with virtues and defects like any other, I also had a lot of friends, a stable relationship but I didn't have something as important as a few millions in the bank.

I was dissatisfied with a lot of situations from my daily life and when one feels this way it generates discontent, anguish and unhappiness. My basic needs were covered, I didn't lack health or food, but I also didn't have everything I wanted or that I believed that I could have.

I had my attention drawn to the fact that tons of people around the world enjoyed ways of living much better than mine and I wanted to have that too. I'll repeat myself: I didn't lack anything essential for my survival, but I had the will to obtain more amenities and liberties (power of intention).

Being conscious and aware of the fact that other people have a better lifestyle and being able to see the reason as to why you can't, is of abundance.

I know it because when I observed them, I wasn't doing it from a place of envy. Quite the opposite, it was out of admiration at seeing so many people with a rich person mindset.

My need of becoming a millionaire changed my way of feeling and thinking. When this hunger of wanting to substantially improve my economic situation was born, at the beginning I saw the lottery as a real and quick way to do it. What

I didn't have in mind was that excessive expectations were making me become overly attached with the results, and not being able to achieve them awakened negative emotions like fear, anxiety, anger and frustration, among others.

Those emotions started dominating several moments in my life, getting me farther away than ever from the abundance that I hoped for. But I don't want to go into that part yet, later on I'll explain that stage of my life where I learned the importance of health.

With my success completed, the millions from the prize not only fattened my bank account, but they also taught me to have a balanced mind, and about what being abundant in health and love was.

In monetary terms, being abundant means giving without expecting anything in return, it's when money stops being the most important thing in your life because you have such a connection to it, that you don't need to work hard to get it, you earn it thanks to the capacity you have in your mind. This doesn't mean that some millionaires don't continue working hard, a lot of them do, but not for the same reason that those who aren't rich do. They do it because it makes them happy.

As most of you, I went through bad experiences in regard to health, love and money. In the next part you will read the story of my evolution, of how an average Joe overcame at an early age the obstacles that our emotions put in front of our path, to start living a life of abundance.

Something that you absolutely need if you wish to reach all of the aspects of abundance, is the right mindset. In my case, even though the prize gave me the final push to achieve it, I started acquiring the mindset needed at the same time that life was teaching me some important lessons. That was a part of aligning with my wish, about the art of allowing. These teachings were of great importance because once I managed to achieve the manifestation of the money, these lessons would help me to be able to enjoy things like health and love. Only then would I be able to affirm that I possess an abundant and prosperous life.

Every blow I took, it was later revealed to have been one more step towards preparing myself for the success of my manifestation that was soon to come. It's also true that some of the obstacles were hard to overcome, I could even admit that during the path towards achieving my wish, I went through the hardest times in my life. If you ask me, I will tell you that, as hard as it was, I wouldn't change a single thing. Those adversities I faced filled me with the strength I needed to now live an abundant and prosperous life. I chose some of the most important moments from my experience, to try and pass on to you and to let you all know that if you are going through a similar thing, those situations can be tests life puts in front of you.

They were put there so once you reach what you yearn for, you can be prepared to be happy with them in the best way.

MONEY

I chose to be rich

"Clear your mind of all strange, negative and super-stitious beliefs about money. Be aware of everything you have learned about money on television, during childhood, with friends or colleagues. Besides making you live a happy and fulfilling life, with the money you can help those who need it "

Dr. Joseph Murphy

No one is afraid to say that they feel lucky about being a person surrounded by loved ones, friends, family or a partner. It's right to be healthy, no one hides they are following a healthy diet or doing exercise that helps them feel and look good. But when we talk about money the opposite happens, we start coming across different opinions.

Money is something that worries people on a daily basis and while it's not the root of happiness, it does contribute to helping us lead the lifestyle that we wish for and the result of it is also happiness.

So, why are privileged people not seen with good eyes most of the time? Why are they the target of criticism from those who can't have the abundance they wish?

For me to win the lottery and to be living the life I wished for, one of the fundamental steps I had to sort through was to completely CHANGE my thoughts about money and wealthy people. I had to recognize that during my educational years I had never acquired teachings orientated towards thoughts of wealthiness, in order to start changing the mindset of fear and shortage.

My intense curiosity led me to be interested in all sorts of materials like books, articles and videos that were related to topics about wealth. I noticed that I was not the only one, and that the vast majority of people in my country didn't have any type of financial education, neither at school nor at home.

In Argentina, people tend to have a mindset that is far from wealthiness, but close to "stability". For example: the ones who go into degrees like Law, have for the most part the same goal of landing a good job working for the State (for this to happen you *need* to have someone on the inside, because no one gets into this type of job on merits alone. The only requirement that matters is to have a dad, mom, uncle, family friend or anyone who has a high position that can lend a hand for these types of favors). A college degree will give you an edge in aiming for the positions at the top of the hierarchy. The exception to the rule is for the more "ambitious" ones who get involved into politics, where standards don't matter much but rather the personal performance you accomplish. I don't have much to object to there, there's a lot of merit involved for those who make it.

That would be a logical and respectable thought process for the mindset of the Argentinian people. It's hard to judge this type of attitude. If we analyze the history of my country, the only ones that have never gone through an economic crisis are the politicians. Throughout the years, they are the only ones who have raised their salaries, with no recession or inflation affecting them. But still, they will sell themselves to the people (voters) acting as if they are the solution to the problems they created. Political parties come and go, and they are never going to step up to the plate to work on the underlying problems, the ones that help to educate people to change their mindset of poverty.

The terrible thing is that the only people who benefit from people with that way of thinking are the politicians and some religions as well. But I'll leave that topic for later.

In this part of the world, that mindset makes few people take the risk of becoming rich in any other way that doesn't involve the state.

We went through so many crises because of their horrendous politics, that nowadays no one thinks about becoming an entrepreneur or to grow on their own merits. People are afraid, afraid of what could happen if they take the risk of starting a business for fear of what they could lose. That's why working in the federal or state governments is an excellent option. In general, these types of jobs don't involve too much responsibility, are well paid and the vacation time is acceptable if we consider that they are just employees. But what is more surprising and that no one sees as a problem is that, when you accept one of these state jobs, you'll get stuck in comfort and you'll never try to leave to chase your dreams or to become a millionaire on your own merit. They aren't temporary jobs, they are forever. Let me tell you a story...

A father and a mother make a career over a 30-year period working for the state. First, they are low-level employees in a town, then they climb up the ladder in such a way that they start occupying more important positions in the city and, in the end, manage to secure an important political position for the state.

By the time they retire, they will have made a sufficient amount of money that will let them, and their kids live comfortably. They never generated any extra money outside of the state, they simply enjoyed many years of great salaries and nowadays they benefit from an excellent retirement.

The children of these parents have the financial possibility (thanks to the stability their parent's money gives them) of choosing to study at university without the need of working at the same time. After getting their degree, they can choose to set up a private law studio, be their own boss and generate income according to their capacity (for better or worse). They also have the privilege of knowing that if they run into trouble and they aren't successful in their profession as solicitors, their parents can always provide a new job in the government thanks to their "contacts".

The mindset of those kids and their parents is one that doesn't even let them try to set up their own law studio. They have the opportunity of trying to be the bosses of their own time, of generating big income and it doesn't even cross their mind to try. From the day they started studying, they did it with the idea of a comfortable government job. And this is the type of mindset that reigns in my country.

I don't want to be a hypocrite, for the longest time I also wished for that life. During my childhood I dreamed about being a football player, but as the years passed, I dismissed that possibility and started yearning to land that type of job for the rest of my life. Luckily, I never had any insider that could help me get any of those jobs, because if I had had one, the comfort would have never allowed me to be interested in the LoA and much less winning the lottery with the conscientious use of the law.

The financial abundance isn't something people usually acquire, it's something you tune in, like I did.

Since I came into this world, money was the protagonist of the most important situations in my life.

In the first years of my life, I had to live in a little town over 186 miles away from the city my family is from. The reason is that my dad had gotten a job from the state that was important, and it was in my family interest for him to take it. It wasn't the most comfortable of things for a number of reasons, but what tipped the scale for my parents to make the decision for him to take the job was that, with that salary, my family could live better than if we stayed in the city. But for the rest of everyday things, it wasn't that practical.

My mother had to take care of me and my three older brothers while my dad spent the whole day working. The town was the typical quiet place where my brothers could play on the street and if that weren't enough, we had a club nearby. Our house was big, with a big backyard where we spent most of our time playing football and running around. My dad was close to his job, so he had the chance to come back to have lunch with us.

In general, the few memories I have of those first years of my life are really good, they were basically my only experience of living in a typical family and my memory chose to pick the best things from those years. But, of course, I was too young and didn't understand that things weren't really going all that well for others.

My mother missed her parents, her friends and the city life in general. My dad's work carried a lot of pressure and gave him a lot of stress that he probably took home. Both my parents had situations that made them feel unhappy living in the town. Which is why, three years and a half after I was born, my family's experience in that town was over. Political problems motivated my dad's resignation and that's how we returned to our native city, this time to start fresh.

As the years went by, things didn't go well for my family. My dad didn't manage to find work stability, my mom took care of us, but the money was never enough. During those first years I lived in three different homes in a lapse of no more than four years until my last grandma (from my mom's side) passed away. That's how we ended up at her house, which happened to be the last thing of economic value my family had left.

The situation didn't get better in the slightest, the mood at home was volatile, day by day we witnessed tension between my parents that sometimes ended with loud arguments, always about how to make ends meet. A couple of years later, the unavoidable happened and my parents split up.

After the breakup, my dad tried to do anything in his power to gives us everything we needed, but he succeeded on very few occasions (if we go by my parent's standards), and that's why he made the decision of moving away (to the capital city of the country) far from us with the idea of getting more promising work opportunities that never came in the end. I remember that all I wanted was for him not to leave, I felt his absence and missed him too much. I would have loved to have had the possibility of sharing more moments from this time of my life with him, but I don't reproach him about anything, I know he had it even harder, as he was away from me and my brothers, but he did it because he wanted what was best for the family. Back then I hated money, I believed it was money's fault that I couldn't be with my dad, I thought about how money had taken him away.

With a father immersed in the hunt for money, away from my daily routine and a mother with emotional problems (logical given the circumstances), caused by the responsibility of bringing up 4 children, my mindset developed.

My brothers and I went to the best Roman Catholic private school in the city, where it was normal to be surrounded with people with a better economic present than us.

This part isn't easy to explain, because while I don't doubt that the intention of our parents was to give us the best education, by not having good support at home, the situation got very awkward.

The scarcity in my home was noticeable when compared to the majority of my classmates and those of my brothers. At that time, because I was young, I didn't understand anything about thoughts and mindsets, but I assure you that the lack, the shortage of things was what influenced me the most.

I had some resentment and anger towards those people around me who lived surrounded by things I couldn't have. I didn't see rich people with good eyes, and I always thought that to have that good financial situation meant that your parents did sketchy things. They were the bad guys, the ones who didn't share and lived without a care for anyone but themselves, always with new shoes, the latest car and dream houses. They went on vacation to places I could only see on TV or in photos. That way of thinking was the one I adopted and grew throughout my growth as a child and as a teenager, with respect to rich people and money.

The last situation that marked the destiny of my family with money was the loss of our home because we were unable to pay the bank the mortgage.

With my dad back living in the city, a bad transaction left us without a home. The one good thing I can find in this situation is that the eviction happened after more than one or two years because of bureaucracy, and by that time my father was back practicing Law and getting more recognized. This made it so we could live in good places (despite them not being our own) and that it became nor-mal for us to move every couple of years. Every time we moved it was to go to a better place, so I'm very thankful for that.

In short, that was the formation of my mindset in regard to money inside the family circle. I would also like to highlight another site that had a big im-pact in helping me build my mindset.

Like the majority of the people from my country, I was baptized in the Roman Catholic Church. This isn't a minor thing, because this religion usually preaches about money in a very particular way. An example of this:

"Above all, try to be free in relation to things. The Lord calls us to an evangelical lifestyle of sobriety, of not letting us get involved with the culture of consump-tion. It's about looking for what's essential, learning to let go of the many superfluous things that drown us into making us want to believe that the materialistic things in this life are important. Let us liberate our-selves from the greed of wanting, of idealized money. Let's put Jesus first. He can liberate us of the idolatries that turn us into slaves. Believe in God, beloved youth! He knows us, loves us and he never forgets us. In the same way he watches over the lilies on the field, he won't let us lack anything. Also, to overcome an eco-nomic crisis there needs to be a will to change the life-style, to avoid splurging" ...

These are words by Pope Francis (first pope from

the Americas, first supreme pontiff of the order of Jesus, born in Flores, Buenos Aires, Argentina), which took place at the inauguration of the World Youth Day 2014. What did you think about them? I won't go into detail criticizing Catholics and their authorities, that's not my intention, but I believe that the speech broadly summarizes how we were raised in regard to faith and money.

I could write some paragraphs with clear examples about my experience during my formative years (14 years) in a catholic school, but as I said before, that's not my intention. I mention this just in case you find similarities with thoughts you believe that have been imposed on you since you were a kid, so you can identify them and make your own conclusions. This way, you'll be in a position to choose different thoughts regarding money and what you can do with it.

A lot of times, without realizing it, we have certain positions in life that were imposed and hammered into us which are harmful if we want to advance and see our desires manifested.

After identifying that there was nothing good in poverty and scarcity, not much time passed until I won the lottery.

Maybe this last part makes you think that I hold a grudge towards the Catholic Church but it's not true. As I learned in Joseph Murphy's book "The Power of your Subconscious Mind", I think that the law of belief operates in a perfect way in all religions thanks to our faith.

Next, I'm going to cite a little fragment from Dr Murphy's book, because besides being fascinated with the content of those words, they help me CLARIFY that I simply criticize the church I was raised in, because I understand that it's an aspect in which the authorities should work on in order to teach their beliefs.

If they help people generate thoughts of abundance, they will come across wealthiness much easier and this will let them help those who don't have the possibility of getting rid of that disease that is the mental state of poverty.

"It isn't the thing believed in that brings an answer to man's prayer; the answer to prayer results when the individual's subconscious mind responds to the mental picture or thought in his mind. This law of belief is operating in all religions of the world and is the reason why they are psychologically true. The Buddhist, the Christian, the Moslem, and the Hebrew all may get answers to their prayers, not because of the particular creed, religion, affiliation, ritual, ceremony, formula, liturgy, incantation, sacrifices, or offerings, but solely because of belief or mental acceptance and receptivity about that for which they pray. The law of life is the law of belief, and belief could be summed up briefly as a thought in your mind. As a man thinks, feels, and believes, so is the

condition of his mind, body, and circumstances. A technique, a methodology based on an understanding of what you are doing and why you are doing it will help you to bring about a subconscious embodiment of all the good things of life. Essentially, answered prayer is the realization of your heart's desire."

Joseph Murphy, The Power of Your Subconscious Mind

A person can and must want to be abundant, the Universe is also abundant, so there's nothing wrong with it, and it's even our right to lead a life full of abundance. Well spent money is helpful, helpful, helpful. On a daily basis, it brings you closer towards happy moments and the ideal life that we dream of.

Nowadays, being in a privileged financial position, I allow myself to say without fear that while my main objective isn't to win money with this book, I don't doubt that I would love it. Making money with this would mean that there are lots of people out there interested in this content, and, if they are, it might be because someone recommended it to them and if that someone recommended it means that some aspect of the book helped them. That means that if it helped them, I would be making money by helping others.

Also, I just confess that I love the feeling of receiving money from different places and putting it into circulation, because the more money I make the more people and animals I can help.

I learned that helping out with money is something fantastic and comforting. I experimented with donating cash to the children's hospital of my city and it's hard for me to explain or describe with words the excitement of the hospital staff when they received the money. Knowing that they are going to be able to buy things they need, like food and equipment that will help them with their daily work with sick kids is a feeling like no other. No matter the good intentions people may have, only those of us who have a sufficient amount of money and decide to share it can do it.

The wonderful thing about becoming a millionaire by winning the lottery is that I didn't make any money at the expense of others or by harming anyone. When you win a lot of money in a game like this one, you know that a good chunk of it goes to the state. 30% (and some more) went to taxes and I would have liked them to let me know which place my money was going to be destined. But I know there's a lot of interest at play and getting an answer would be almost impossible.

My only job was living life and while I did this, I aligned myself with what I was yearning (the lottery) for. I didn't need advice, I didn't spend my whole life studying or working, I simply asked for it, the LoA was the vehicle and the Universe guided me, it threw obstacles in front of me (changes) to be prepared for when my wish was granted. I learned and I always acted in a proper way for my desire to manifest.

Free yourself from guilt

Like most people, I didn't receive adequate training to help me build a mindset of wealth at a young age, but now that I do, I can tell you that I don't hold hard feelings at all against my family or teachers, on the contrary, I am grateful to all of them. I thank them for helping me in the best way they could during the years I was developing as a person. I learned values, to read, write and interpret, and that was enough for me to gain curiosity and understand that there was nothing wrong with being rich, and that in reality, it was something extremely positive.

This restlessness led me to go and acquire knowledge on my own, which led to the construction of a wealth mentality. The basis for transforming the foundations of my mentality was the feeling of gratitude, of being truly grateful for all the experiences I have gone through throughout my life and finally freeing myself from the guilt. This is the way I began to eliminate the resentment I had with many situations and people in my life, which evidently didn't allow me to go on with my work of aligning myself with my desire to become a millionaire.

I started becoming a more spiritual being of faith, in a person who found reasons to be grateful on a daily basis which meant that I felt happiness in my day-to-day life.

Then I started incorporating knowledge about finances, economics, investments and what I would do in the moment when I received a significant sum of money. This is how my mindset abruptly changed and gave way for me to receive my wish.

Money does buy happiness

Strictly speaking about material things, one of the best ways to help others is to have a solid economy. I wish everyone would experience the wonderful feeling of helping with money and to realize that sometimes good gestures and attitudes are just not enough.

Imagine how happy you can make a loved one with a simple envelope containing the airline tickets to go to the place they have always dreamt of going and hadn't had the chance to visit because they didn't have enough money. Imagine telling your mom to go with you to the grocery store and in the middle make a stop to hand her the keys to a new car. Or seeing a friend in a bad mood, because he has trouble paying the rent of his business, then, after being with him, you get up and go to the real estate agency and pay three months of rent in advance, plus the ones he owed. This way, you manage to alleviate what until that moment was a problem that was difficult to solve for a loved one.

Perhaps you think that these are temporary solutions and on a certain point you are right, because if the mindset of the person you help is one of scarcity, surely in a short time, they will return to the same place they were before receiving your help. That's why the help of material things is so important. Words are also a big help because knowing how to convey thoughts of abundance is of extreme importance. And I put emphasis on this when someone makes room to receive advice.

Before I helped him with the rent, my friend had been interested in taking advice on what had led to my financial success, and it wasn't about how to guess the lottery numbers, but about the way I changed my way of thinking to have been able to manifest the lottery.

I felt grateful for being listened to and the fact that he accepted books that would help him transform his mindset. He placed great value on the knowledge acquired in those readings and the interest generated, led him to watch videos and acquire information from other sources.

Sometime later, with what he was able to save on rent thanks to my financial help and his change of mindset, in just a few months he successfully reinvented his business, to the point that sales are making him see the possibility of opening a new branch and generating income that months ago seemed impossible.

The most important piece of advice I gave him was to stop blaming the country's economic situation for the lack of sales of his business. I explained to him that regardless of the circumstances, there is always a way to be successful. The key isn't to start blaming (in this case the government) that only end up creating grudges, and to seek out a way he could reinvent the business to keep it afloat.

I understand that, in Latin American countries like Venezuela, the situation can be much more complex, but there is a universal truth that doesn't exclude anyone and that is that, if you anchor yourself in resentment and guilt, it's almost a fact that you won't move forward to achieve the ideal of life you wish for.

I would like you to take a few minutes to think, to imagine and to feel right now, about what you would buy or about who you would help if you had a lot of money... Don't be afraid, start creating positive emotions and give life to the intention of being financially abundant because I can assure you that regardless of the situation or the country you are in, it's possible.

Fill your head with thoughts of abundance, meditate, visualize everything you want to achieve, manifest your intention, act and the Universe, God or life will put the tools in your hands to achieve that ideal of life that you deserve. Erase any traces of scarcity from your mind and success will not take long to arrive. It didn't take long to come for me and I'm no different from you. I believe that you can do it too.

Perhaps your dreams are about achieving financial abundance by other means, you can't lie to yourself. Analyze my experience and see what similarities or differences you find with your desire to be a millionaire and put them into practice. I want to clarify that, if I hadn't won the lottery, I have no doubt that in some way I would have still achieved economic abundance, and it's not my intention to be arrogant, I'm being totally honest. I already felt the wealth within me, my thoughts were in tune and the lottery was the focus point where I really put my attention to achieve it.

There are infinite ways to make money and the way in which people become millionaires these days is far from how it was years ago. The world changed and financial abundance now comes to people doing what they love, those who stand out in an activity because of their passion and dedication.

The time when only those who had professional degrees, athletes or business owners were the only ones who could aspire to earn a ton of money has passed.

The world is connected in many ways and global-ized communication gives the possibility of gen-erating abundance in an infinite number of ways. Look inside yourself, maybe there, where your pas-sions lay, is the key to finding financial abundance, FREEDOM. But I can assure you that, if you don't change the way you think about money and those who have it in large quantities, it's going to be diffi-cult for you to manifest a change in your life.

Maybe you won't end world hunger, but I also don't think it's something that depends solely on you. If in addition to helping your family, friends you also go out and collaborate with someone you don't even know without a doubt, you are already doing a lot. You are giving without expecting anything back, and that is what having a mindset of wealth means.

Being in a privileged economic position gives you the option to choose and when you choose to do good by sharing part of your wealth to help others and that generates emotions of happiness, you'll have come to understand everything.

Lastly, please don't think that I am encouraging everyone to leave their jobs and go out like crazy to do what they love, obviously that would not be a very appropriate thing to do. But please dedicate some time to that activity you believe can help you come closer to having economic abundance into your life. If you love it, you won't take it as a job or burden, and it will make you vibrate in the frequency of happiness and when you are on that tune is when the odds of winning the lottery are sky-high. Situated in that vibrational frequency (happiness) is when the magic happens.

When I aligned myself with the frequency of the lottery, allowing it to flow towards me, I experienced the amazing sensation of materializing many of the things that I had already felt as my own, during the visualizations of over a year. Now came the time to go shopping ...

My promised gifts

What I'm going to share with you now is simply a narration of what I bought during those first days as a millionaire. I do this humbly and with the goal of motivating you. I would like that while you read, visualize and feel what you would do if you received millions from one day to the next.

I had told myself that if one day I could manifest a good sum of money in the lottery, I would not let anyone tell me what to buy and not to buy. I understand that these words may sound ugly, but believe me, there is nothing wrong with that.

I had been developing a wealth mentality for a long time, and the fact that I didn't indulge myself, believing that these indulgences could come to become too expensive, was part of a scarcity mindset that was no longer a part of me. Mind you, I'm not saying that I quickly spent all my money or that I gave myself super extravagant luxuries, not at all.

Part of the preparation to let my desire flow perfectly towards me, was to study the investments that I would make when all the money arrived, although for logistical reasons, it was easier to give myself some treats first, before putting the money to work for me.

The home

The first gift I gave myself was my apartment. To be honest this isn't really a fabulous story by any means, but I do think it has an incredible or magical touch.

The choice was very simple. It was thanks to the fact that, as I told you, I had everything meticulously studied. I knew its price, who sold it and every detail that might arise during the purchase operation. That's what you should do if you want to manifest something so incredibly big and not ruin it, so PREPARE FOR THE MOMENT.

Once I had the lottery check deposited into my account, the first thing I did was to dial the seller's phone number, set up a meeting, and close the deal a few days later.

I made sure it had a beautiful view of nature, something which is an essential thing in my life. I love waking up and going to sleep, gazing at the view of the rivers and trees that my city has. They elevate me during my meditations and generate good vibes inside of me throughout the day.

The detail that cemented the operation is that the apartment I was buying had been the same one that they had shown me months before when I had gone to see the place. But, of course, at that time I didn't even have 1% of the value of the apartment. I had agreed to go see it with the intention that when I visualized it, I would feel it more deeply, using real images.

That day they could have shown me any of the 30+ flats, but they just happened to show me the 9th floor one. When I came back, with the money to carry out the transaction, they showed me the same apartment. They told me that a person had bought it as an investment, but that until now he had never wanted to rent it or sell it.

It's magical and incredible to think that during the course of time in which I was preparing for the manifestation of my wish, the apartment didn't have any type of movement. Without a doubt it was there, as if waiting for me. When I had seen it for the first time, I had noticed each one of the details. I had taken photographs which I kept on my cell phone to look at them once in a while and when they handed me the keys and I walked in as the owner...nothing had changed. The only thing that (gladly) changed was that this time the photos that I took were from and in my own apartment.

The car

The next purchase was the car. To buy a brand-new one I had to travel to a city 100 miles away from where I lived, since in my city there is no official dealership for that brand. Ferrari? Lamborghini? Maserati? No, not at all. In my city there isn't a single car of any of those brands and it would have been totally unwise and unsafe to have them. It was a Mini Cooper. Maybe it wasn't a super luxurious car or maybe in your country they are quite common. But it was the car of my dreams, the vehicle that I had always wanted and had never been able to buy. I loved all of the models, the trucks, the sporty ones, the Clubman... all of them, and all the colors seemed fantastic to me.

Months before, I had done something similar to the apartment with the car. It's just that the visualization with the real images of what one desires, is an extraordinary way of producing positive deep emotions.

On a few occasions (for work reasons), I traveled to that city and had the audacity to go to the dealership to get inside the car to get a feel of it. I hadn't done the test drive, but I was able to immerse myself in several of them. I felt the smell, the different gear transmissions, the multifunction steering wheels, the sound coming out of the speakers and other details in order to make the most accurate visualizations.

You may think that it makes no sense to do this type of practice, like going to see a car or apartment without having the money to buy them. If that is what you think, you must work hard on your faith. Don't feel ashamed, because firstly; it's a feeling of very low vibration and secondly; because believe me when I tell you that this type of practice helps our subconscious to find a way to manifest those things. Look at this tool, as a support to acquire more confidence and firmness for the accuracy of your visualizations.

In the case of the car, when I visualized it, I did it effectively, with all my senses well sharpened with its smell, the noise of its ignition, the music that would come out of those fabulous speakers, the touch with its new automatic transmission, the lights reflecting off the floor when the doors were opened. Every detail was perfectly reproduced by my imagination in the visualizations. As of today, I can say that I enjoy it almost daily feeling deeply grateful for it. I'm far from seeing it as something that became a habit not worthy to continue being excited about. That is why I put a lot of emphasis on being prepared to receive because if I had won the lottery before I was ready, I would have surely quickly grown tired of these material things, but since that wasn't the case, my feelings of gratitude are daily and that tunes me alongside happiness, allowing me to continue growing.

The act of going to the car dealership and getting on some cars cleared my mind and confirmed that I really wanted it, because it's one thing to just see them on the street and quite another to feel it from the inside.

I swear to you that I find it difficult to put into words the feelings running through me the day I drove the car around the first couple of streets. The amount of happiness that invaded my body was so big, that at the first traffic light I stopped, I let out a scream of YEEEEEEESSSSSSSSSSS!!!!!!!! from deep within my soul.

Leisure

While waiting for my new gifts to be delivered, I put together a schedule of three trips that I would make the next year, each one of them with the people who helped me stay positive and happy during my changes throughout the course of the manifestation process. All especially thought and designed in accordance with the tastes of the people who would accompany me in mind, without going over any details and giving free rein to all the luxury and comfort that was within my reach. I was not afraid to spend too much, I knew that for that year my well-studied investments would leave me good royalties. And so it happened.

Investments

I live in a country where inflation and the rise

of the dollar are the protagonists of the economy year after year. Although this is a problem for the vast majority of Argentines, it is true that making money this way can be easier.

On the path towards the transformation to the wealth mindset, I learned that, if you want to get rich, you have to eliminate any type of excuses and to stop blaming third parties. This includes blaming the country you were born in and the way the politicians govern it.

The prize I obtained when I won the lottery was millions of Argentine pesos. The amount doesn't even reach the one-million-dollar figure, which is why my financial preparation to know where and how to invest was essential.

Once I had the check deposited in my account, it was my turn to put the recently acquired knowledge into practice, so that, with that figure, I could start to have the lifestyle I had been yearning for.

As I told you, I didn't buy a super luxurious car, nor a mansion because If I had, that would have been a huge mistake. Instead, I chose to buy the vehicle I had always loved, without it being extremely expensive or flashy, I didn't even go for one of the most expensive brand models but rather one of the cheapest. When I want to drive an extravagant car with those characteristics, I rent it in some city in the USA, where they don't attract so much attention and their costs are affordable.

The first investment I made was in real estate outside of Argentina, so that I can get an entry of money in a strong, stable currency that doesn't depreciate. That way I would never be dependent on the situation my country goes through and, if this were to happen, I would possibly even benefit from it, since every month I would be cashing in a different currency. It's hard to say, but it's the truth. With that first investment I made sure to be subjected to the economic setbacks that we have in this part of the world.

Now it was my turn to invest in something that I liked and that was within the scope in the city. That way I could keep myself busy and motivated thinking about growing the business. That is why the second investment was destined towards a food and health business in partnership with some friends who had already been working in the field. Our idea is to establish in the city, and then to go out into the region and the world. This endeavor is a great success because while I have the absolute conviction and I have faith that we are going to do great, regardless of the results, I get to work in an environment where there is a high positive energy circulating constantly, alongside my friends who see life in a very similar way to how I see it.

This job is really enjoyable, I don't see it as a burden, I don't have pressures and the responsibilities are in accordance with the activities that I take pleasure in doing. As a group, we constantly support and motivate each other (as a true work team), to overcome any obstacles that arise and to achieve the goals that we set ourselves.

The third and last investment I made as soon as I received the prize money, also took place in my city and with my girlfriend. Before I won the award, she owned a business that was running very well, but after we invested a considerable amount of money, the sales blew up quickly. The business was booming. She works at the place and is in charge of everything that has to do with the daily occurrences of the business, while I handle the administrative part. In that sense, we continue to evolve and grow together.

In conclusion, the jackpot was sufficient so that, with my mentality and training, I could lead the lifestyle that I always wanted. It's true that a quick and sudden fortune in the hands of an incapable individual would probably destroy them. But that wasn't my case. With faith, I spent many hours training myself for when financial abundance came to me, to be prepared so this isn't something temporary, but an opportunity to make more money. *This is how I think and how I act.*

As of today, I CAN AFFIRM THAT I AM ABUNDANT AND PROSPEROUS.

LOVE

"In an ideal world, each person would be free to start a relationship whenever they wanted, with someone who really complemented and respected them. A healthy relationship can be very beneficial for a person since it opens the doors to a series of experiences impossible to experience alone. And while it's not correct to generalize and it is true that some enjoy not sharing their lives, others feel that as a pair everything is easier, everything is more enjoyable; for the latter, this means that having their better half is an invaluable gift".

Definition of relationship, according to the dictionary

Starting off from this accurate definition, whatever your current emotional state may be, you must learn to respect and love yourself in the first place. This is one of the keys if we want to manifest a big change, such as earning a lot of money in a short period of time, or if what we want to find is a good partner to have in our lives. Because, although they seem different things or that don't have much in common, being financially abundant can be closely related to being well on the sentimental aspect. That was my case.

To raise our vibrational frequency in such a way that allows us to manifest our desires, it's crucial that we know how to love and respect ourselves.

Loving and respecting myself was a very important starting point to accommodate my life for the manifestation of the lottery. But before receiving my wish, or rather, before even setting up that goal, the journey of learning began by knowing how to love and respect myself, for later, without even having planned it, finding an excellent partner.

There are many who think that the mixture of love and money don't go well together, but I prefer to state the opposite. Thanks to the fact that I found a partner, I was able to put myself together (sentimentally speaking). That was a key piece of the puzzle to help me be successful with money.

I changed my way of thinking about money and wealthy people, and I did the same with my love life. First of all, I learned to love myself, and then once I found a partner, I knew how to carry a relationship and evolve with it.

Usually when starting a relationship what happens is that at first, we want to spend as much time as possible with our partner with the predominant feelings being excitement, tolerance and affection. That is why the differences that may exist between the two are either not noticed or left aside for fear of getting into discussions that could put an end to that happy feeling of infatuation.

After a while, those aspects that we relinquished at

the beginning, if we don't acknowledge and work on them, will turn into trouble or into something that can be even worse, tedium.

I used to be the type of person that, in order to be okay with my partner, did things I was not comfortable with, which is something that could be considered "normal" because when you decide to be with someone, it's only fair and logical to cede on some aspects. The problem is that, if we get used to living this way, we'll end up losing our essence and find ourselves thinking that we like the things we do, when in reality it's not that we like them, but that we got used to things developing in this manner. The result of this is that not only do we fail to identify the problem, but we also end up doing things that aren't conducive to our well-being and that make us vibrate at a low frequency with regularity.

If we find the problem, we would be in a position to find a way to solve it, because if we don't, over time it will create a feeling of unhappiness.

When we let feelings that aren't in the best interests of our well-being grow inside of us, we give way to unwanted emotions such as intolerance, anger, fear, shame, jealousy, anxiety and depression (among others). All because we were not being honest with ourselves and with our partner.

When one is involved in a relationship, at the same time that the relationship progresses, it's the most normal thing for it to do so leaning to the side of becoming accustomed and not on the side of looking to evolve together.

Evolution would be to be able to build a strong commitment, to see the best teammate in the other person, to value the other person more deeply, practicing at having an attentive and understanding emotional bond that enriches both parties equally.

Knowing when to say "yes" and when to say "no", without it affecting the relationship. We identify that with the feeling, if we do many things without liking them, just in the name of satisfying the other person, or for fear of getting into a fight, then that means that we are in a relationship inclined towards the side of accustoming, which isn't exactly what happiness is. This is the main thing that factors in wearing down and eventually leading to a breakup. This is as long as someone doesn't realize that they aren't happy and has the courage to make the decision of letting the relationship go. Unfortunately getting accustomed includes not knowing how and when to let go and the predominant emotion in those cases is fear.

When I manifested the lottery, it was not by chance that I was going through a wonderful and happy relationship, far from being accustomed and constantly evolving. And I'm not saying that I have a perfect relationship by no means, we obvi-

IGNACIO TORRES

ously have our fights and crises, but despite those discussions or disagreements, we are clear about where we are and where we want to go.

One of the key reasons why I think my sentimental relationship evolves is that I actually learned to say "YES" and "NO". Always respecting my partner, caring for her and accompanying her in everything she believes is for her own good and that doesn't negatively affect me. The fact that I have no problem saying "no", even if it seems otherwise, is extremely positive. She knows them well and appreciates my noes. Knowing how to use them and how to interpret them is an important part in building an honest and long-lasting relationship. Acting in such a way I am true to myself and to her.

I had an idea of how to identify toxic emotions because some time ago I had suffered through them, partly due to the lack of knowledge and power that self-love brings.

After ending a decade old relationship, I experienced painful situations due to my lack of self-esteem. The women I showed interest in, quickly distanced themselves away from me, as a result of the intensity I radiated.

During that period of time, I went through very painful moments, to the point that I considered that some of them had been humiliating. I would later learn that they were valuable life lessons for which I should be grateful; because as with all mistakes and failures, if you know how to learn from them, then those lessons will always be positive.

I used to be "in love" (or so I thought) with a woman whose tastes had little to do with mine, but without realizing it and to please her, I started acting as someone I wasn't. I went to places where I didn't feel comfortable, I ate foods that I didn't like, I hung out with people she considered as *cool*, but for me they were the opposite. I laughed at things that I didn't find funny to me and stopped doing all kinds of activities that *I did like*, because I was terrified at the idea that she would walk away from me.

The turning point was when I caught her making out with another man inches away from me at a nightclub. Want to hear something strange? I didn't end things with her right there at that very moment. Instead of making a break for it and getting as far away from her as I could, I incredibly kept seeking her out for *weeks* begging her for her love. The only thing that was clear in that situation was *my lack of self-love*. I didn't have any respect for myself, nor did I take care of my own person and I pretended to have other people do it for me. My feelings and needs were of little to no importance to a person that I thought of as the most important to me. I couldn't find an answer and I dumped on myself. I saw myself as ugly, useless and incapable of being loved.

During those days, I relapsed into blaming others and to bring forth past situations and attribute them for my bad mood. I didn't pay attention to myself and to the way I was acting. I had made one of the biggest mistakes that a human being can make in regard to love by letting my mood be exclusively dependent on another person. If she wanted to be with me or to see me, I was over the moon, but if, on the contrary, she decided to distance herself, I crumbled. This affected my work, my relationship with my family, friends and with my sleep. I couldn't sleep at all, and this led me to make the decision, being under 30, to start taking sleeping pills.

Do you see how terrible this can turn into? Do you realize how complicated your life can become, if your happiness depends solely on how someone else feels about you? ... You should never, EVER, let this happen to you.

My experience and the ones of many other people or renowned authors who talk about these topics, opened my eyes and helped me to understand that a partner should be someone that complements your happiness, and that your happiness should never be 100% dependent on what another person feels about you.

We as people are constantly changing and if for some reason that is foreign to you, someone decides not to continue their life by your side, you should never crumble.

If you do, you would be losing something as valuable as your self-love and when this happens, you lose the respect and even the affection of that many people that surround you. Not only are you risking the chance of losing the possibility of meeting someone new but also for your friends or family, you go from being company to "a burden". You turn into someone people have to "put up with", who rants against everyone for being unlucky in love. And that, logically, affects your relationships, friendships, your work and all aspects of your life.

If you continue to drown in your own pain, as a consequence, you'll generate a contained anguish that will transform into an anger that will harm you and those around you. Don't let negative experiences affect the way you relate to people.

The more you desire to surpass yourself and heal your interior, the better prepared you will be to collect more strength which with to keep going forward

Bernardo Stamateas

Accustoming

After spending many long nights because of an unrequited love, I realized that what I was looking to replicate was that state of engagement, the feeling of being loved or important to someone. Internally I wanted to have a repeat of that habit that meant doing everything as a couple. Back then, the person didn't matter much, as soon as I liked a woman (without even knowing her), I went all out for her, to the point of neglecting myself and completely forgetting the value of self-love.

You must find a balance when giving your energy to another person so what happened to me doesn't also occur to you. With this method, you won't forsake yourself and you will gain self-knowledge. Someone who loves themselves is someone who respects themselves and makes themselves be respected, they know their worth and the others also know it.

Instead of collapsing, I decided to get out of that situation. With the help of friends and by reading books, watching videos, taking care of my nutrition and starting to exercise, I made the decision to move on and push forward. I was beginning to understand that I had put myself in that situation and so I had to get myself out of it. I identified that I had been the problem and that my actions were the ones that were going to pull me away from this painful situation.

I was given the first push by books and videos that motivated me to take the first steps. A few months after that bad experience, I improved my physical and mental aspects, revealing my intentions of leading a better life.

It didn't take long for me to start attracting good

things, since my life no longer depended on someone else's mood, or in the way that person treated me, my life depended wholly on ME. As I started gaining confidence, I began to go out with friends, to travel, I improved at work and without looking for it, I found a partner who makes me feel happy and free. Free in the sense that with her I'm truly me, I don't go around pretending to be someone else to please her. She knows what I like, and I know what she likes, we don't try making anything that would compromise us in any way, we don't exert ourselves in any shape or form.

When you get to experience this kind of evolution, you find the true pleasures of life. I choose to share my life with her because I believe that she is a complement that enhances my everyday happiness. She knows my worth and I'm aware of her value. If one day due to life circumstances, she chooses a different path, I won't collapse as a house of cards, *not this time.* I could possibly be sad, but this time I'll have with me my self-love to continue evolving and attracting all the good things this life has to offer.

Understand how loving and respecting yourself will grant you what you desire. Sometimes this happens fast, other times it takes time, but if you love and respect yourself, you will always end up in your desired situation.

As a couple or on your own, depending on how

you prefer to spend your life to feel fulfilled on the sentimental aspect, you must be willing to do something that many never do. YOU MUST MAKE YOURSELF THE PRIORITY, after all, you are the protagonist of your life so make your life a successful movie.

Way too many people still don't know the value, the importance that loving oneself has. When I refer to the phrase "love yourself" I'm not doing it from a narcissistic point of view of thinking about yourself as the most skillful, the wisest or the strongest. Loving yourself means also making yourself be respected and to put a limit to situations that are unfair, unnecessary or that aren't worth wasting your time to address. It's giving good nutrients to the body, giving gifts, pampering and taking care of yourself in every type of way you can think of.

For many years now, we have valued certain things that may not be correct. Hanging on to a relationship is something to be valued in some way, sustaining intolerable situations is valued, from an objective point of view because a lot of love is felt. Do you really think that's love? I think it is being accustomed, something that we often confuse with love. It's a known thing that people can get used to both the good and the bad, for example: you can live in either a mansion or a small home, you can drive a fashionable car or one that only you know the tricks to start it, whatever your choice was or what the circumstances are, with time, you'll get used to it.

In love something similar happens, you get used to a certain type of relationship and then, depending on the way it was shaped into, time starts to become "routine". You get used to certain ways of being treated, complaints, infidelities and by not putting a limit on them they start to pile up and they become a part of your life. They transform into a common occurrence that you didn't wish for, but that at some point you allowed to happen.

There are break-ups that even if at the moment you can't see them, they free you, take away weight of your shoulders, allow you to reunite with yourself and to be you again

Waldo Casal

So, if you think that you are giving yourself away without measure in relationships, if you believe that you are forgetting your needs, or that you don't know how to say "no", let them go, otherwise you'll end up becoming a toxic person to yourself, believing that the toxic person is the other person.

When you need to decide, identify what is the correct response that will make you feel happy and let yourself be guided by that emotion. Remember that if you're feeling well, you'll attract everything you want, be it a partner, health or winning the lottery. But if you go through life just suffering you will hardly attract something that is magnificent for your life.

One of the best ways to vibrate high and allow our desires to flow towards us is with the feeling of love activated.

Unconditional love exists and it occurs when we detach ourselves from all kinds of results, and we see what we love as it truly is, without the need of wanting to perfect it. I find this type of love in my dog, the amount of happiness that we generate between the two of us with only our company makes it so no matter what happens, we are together until the end of this life. I can also find this kind of love in my daughter, my parents and my brothers, because despite the mistakes that we may make, forgiveness will allow me to have unconditional love when it comes to them.

As for me, I can't say that I find this type of love in a partner, not because I don't want to give or receive unconditionality, but because as I already say, I understand that by nature, as human beings we are inconsistent and ever changing and that the choice of who we have as partners, can be modified by the decisions or actions of any of the parties.

And it's not that I am not willing to forgive, but that even if I sincerely forgive a partner, I don't think I could ever feel the same, if I feel like the person acted in such a way that would cause me great harm.

Unconditional love in couples can be quite toxic, as it allows people to do anything they want because they know that they will be forgiven and they'll continue to stay together forever. So, in these cases, I prefer choosing to have conditional love with my partner, whom I choose on a daily basis, without getting too far ahead and with a lot of respect for her.

I also believe that being in a relationship is an excellent way for us to bring out our greatest virtues as humans as it gives us the possibility of living unique experiences. Although the reality is that we must be aware that it can end at any time, for these same reasons. If it no longer vibrates with you, if you no longer flow, if you feel that you aren't moving forward, that is no longer your place.

A partner should be a beautiful complement that contributes to happiness

Never let your happiness be totally dependent on anyone. Instead, give them the possibility to contribute to your well-being and contribute to theirs, but remember never give away full control of your happiness.

When you think of giving yourself away without measure, remember not to lose yourself, don't forget your needs, of the emotions that make you happy, don't believe for a second that you can't say "no". The noes are necessary for both of you. It's true that their use is associated with negative thoughts since "if I say 'no' to him, he will think that I no longer love him or he will stop loving me". The reality is that sometimes, a "no" is the best gift that we can give to our partner and to ourselves. This way of acting will guide you to a more sincere, honest and long-lasting relationship (if you want it) in favor of evolution.

If you don't have a partner and your desire is to find someone who reciprocates your love because you believe that's the way your life would be more complete and that you would be happier, then work hard on yourself, on your self-love and don't try to force the moment, this is how the ideal situation appear in your path. The result will be perfect and your "lack" of searching will bring you closer to someone like you

One thing that is common is that, on more than one occasion, we attract similar relationships with different people into our lives. That is the answer that we attract what we are and that what is presented to us. This is what we pay the most attention to. This is why it's important to be able to identify our strengths and weaknesses, as well as the strengths and weaknesses of the other person. This way of proceeding will prevent us from falling back into past errors, since knowledge will give us the possibility of identifying them in time to correct them, understanding that these situations led us to an unwanted moment or place.

Everything you want is out there waiting for you to ask. Everything you want also wants you. But you have to take action to get it

Jack Canfield

HEALTH

Knowing that every situation carries a message for our evolution, brings magic back to life. It gives it meaning. It doesn't make it easy, it makes it magical

Jorge Schubert

The last of the necessary fundamental pillars that we must consider to enjoy a life of abundance and prosperity is health.

I am a person who, even before knowing about the LoA, had always enjoyed good health. I had never had any major inconvenience about it and to be honest it wasn't something that I valued or felt privileged to have. I didn't include it in my meditations, it wasn't on my visualization board, when I read books that talked about health, I just skipped them. I thought it was something I had and that was it, I wasn't interested in delving much into it.

One Sunday during the period where I was "fully dedicated towards winning the lottery", already with more knowledge and time dedicated to the LoA, with the lottery draw taking place, my spirits were through the roof.

My girlfriend, who lived with me, decided to spend the day at her mom's house, so from early morning until sunset, I was alone in the apartment. I started the day off cleaning my home as there was a lot of disorder and I didn't like seeing the place where I lived in those conditions. When I finished,

I lit a green candle on a table that I have in a corner of the dining room and with the peace of mind that the spotless house gave me, I began to meditate.

Throughout that day, until my girlfriend came back, I did approximately 3 deep guided meditations, with the sole objective of them helping me win in the night's draw.

I can say that I had a very comforting day, full of peace and spirituality, because both during the meditations as well as the rest of the day, I had positively charged feelings that fed my great illusion of becoming a millionaire on that very same night. But the Universe had other plans in the short term for me. Without knowing it, I was hours away from receiving a great lesson. Believing in the possibility of being the winner of millions in a short time, I obtained a lesson that was another piece in the cogwheel to continue developing my evolution.

When my girlfriend came back, we went out to buy some food. Being a hot summer Sunday, we were tempted with cold sandwiches for dinner and ice cream for dessert. We came back from shopping, quickly ate our sandwiches and settled on the couch to start watching a movie, while we had some of that delicious ice cream.

No more than 15 minutes into the movie, I started to feel strange, my hands were sweating and I felt a great pressure on my head, my vision was blurred, everything was confusing, I thought I was going crazy. The vital signs showed that my body was in a state of emergency. I was experiencing for the first time what is commonly referred to as a "panic or anxiety attack".

Fearful of the new sensations, I went to the bathroom to take a shower, believing that I would regain my normal state, but this didn't happen. I came out of the bathroom and still felt the same way. My girlfriend, worried and not knowing what to do, called a friend of mine, who minutes later came to my apartment along with another friend. Still tormented and very fearful, I began to tell him everything I felt, I told them that I thought I was going crazy, that I could not control my thoughts, I even told them that I wanted to commit suicide, but that I didn't do it because I didn't want anyone to suffer for me. Luckily, their company helped me to calm down little by little. With great restraint, after several minutes, one of my friends who is a very spiritual individual, told me something I will never forget. They were the right kind of words at the right time: "calm down, you are changing your state of consciousness and it is something positive".

At that moment I didn't see it that way, I really believed that I would not be able to regain my sanity, I felt absolutely crazy, out of my mind, I didn't control my thoughts at all. What happened to me was that I was going through an extremely rare and unwanted situation, created by the disproportionate expectations that I would become a millionaire through the lottery thanks to the use of LoA.

It was no coincidence that the feeling of anxiety took hold of me on a day which had been completely dedicated to the fulfillment of my wish. It was a Sunday, a draw day and my body and my mind knew it. They also knew that it was approximately 10:00 p.m. and since the draw was at 9:00 p.m., due to the speed with which information is handled today, if there was someone from my city who was the winner of the jackpot, I would have found out about it. But it didn't happen. No one had called me and everything was normal. Anxiety had first taken a hold of my mind and then attacked some parts of my body, through discomfort.

As one of my friends had already experienced some similar episodes of anxiety, he was very well informed of the situation. Although he isn't a professional in the field, that night he acted as one. He didn't transmit fear to me, he calmed me down by speaking clearly, slowly and he helped me breathe little by little in the best way. He also changed my focus out of the situation and normalized it by talking to me about pleasant things. He put funny videos on TV that lessened my distress and appeased the "insanity."

After a few hours, my friends, seeing that I was at ease, decided to leave so I could rest. I went to bed, still with some fear from all the bad emotions that anxiety made me experience. It took me a long time to fall asleep, but finally, thanks to company and the tranquility that my girlfriend provided for me, I was able to do it.

The next day, I woke up quite confused, but luckily, I was much calmer. My breathing was normal, there was neither sweat nor pain of any kind, so the first thing I did (as always) was to go for a walk with my dog.

It was the middle of the morning and the oppressive heat that my city tends to have in summer was still not noticeable. This propelled me to walk for a long time while I reconstructed the events of the previous night in my head. I remembered that at the time of the "attack", I didn't care at all about the lottery, or the benefits that it would bring to my life in case of winning. I wanted to feel good, I wanted to be at peace again.

I realized that, if I weren't in good health, having a lot of money would be of little use to me, it seems so obvious and even trite, but as Thomas Fuller says: "Health isn't valued till sickness comes" and that's exactly what happened to me.

I needed to find an answer for the changes that I was beginning to undergo, the situation had planted questions in my head that I had to analyze.

From then on, everything was different, my life changed and I began to value my health above all. At first, I went to see a psychologist for a few sessions, but I, more than anyone else, knew what the origin was and how to deal with my problem.

The episode made me realize that if I enjoyed good health, I would have lots of ways to make money. The lottery was something that might or might not come to me, so I decided it would be best to let go. But beware, when I said let go, I was not saying that I gave up my desire, I just abruptly changed its importance in my life.

The way I saw my desire changed. I started to become aware that it was not up to me to determine the times of its manifestation. My task or that of all the people who want to consciously benefit from LoA, is to dream big and make a plan of action to see what we want accomplished. From that point of view, a desire such as winning the lottery may sound somewhat contradictory to this assessment, but it is only contradictory if it's expected to be successful quickly and without bothering to make the effort of aligning yourself with your wish by avoiding or without giving relevance to the events around us. That's when we go straight into making a big and common mistake in these cases, which is to expect making a very large vibrational jump, in a short period of time without making any change.

Although it's unclear if it's impossible to achieve it, the reality is that, in that way, there are many details that may not have been within our reach to be able to handle them, they aren't part of a plan of action (something useful to have in our heads).

As a consequence, waiting for immediate results, triggered by the expectations of being the winner of millions from one day to the next, what happens is that the wish never manifests and we end up frustrated week after week to the point of getting sick, like it happened to me.

Acting this way, we would be accessing thoughts and feelings that are far from our current vibrations, generating emotions that take us away from the manifestation of our desires because they make us feel bad. The idea is to make small changes that make us feel good in our daily life, trying to enjoy the process. And if something happens that wasn't in our plans, let you learn from it and use it as knowledge in favor of your evolution and personal growth. Let us detach ourselves from the result of what we want (in my case winning the lottery). In the case of the lottery, the best way to achieve this is to have other projects in mind, to occupy our time and also to supply us with expectation and happiness.

When I understood this, I kept incorporating changes and insights into my mindset. But not only did I change my way of thinking or my faith, but I also changed my actions.

Among all the changes I made, the one that stood out was that I stopped playing a big quantity of tickets. Only sometimes did I play my usual numbers. During my meditations or when I got up and went to sleep, they no longer played a leading role. That role was occupied by my health. I had felt firsthand and in a very real way what it was like to be unhealthy. It was horrible. Imagine telling your girlfriend or friends from one moment to the next that you no longer want to live, that you want to jump off a 10-story building. This is how I came to feel.

I am thankful that I never had an attack of that magnitude again, although fear and anguish were a part of my life for a few more months.

And it's really not easy to overcome anxiety. Because even though the episode was a one-time thing, the fact that it was an unprecedented experience left me extremely worried and fearful during the following months. Several nights and for no reason, I felt depressed. They were moments or instants in which I could not find motivation, I had forgotten about how the small details also contributed to happiness (something beyond the amount of money that my desire could bring)

At first, the stage after the panic attack made me lose a bit of faith and discouraged me about the possibility of manifesting the lottery. I was so sure that I was going to achieve it in a short time, that I forgot the importance of the vibrational frequencies which are a part of the third step explained by the Hicks masters, *the art of allowing it to flow towards you.*

If the result of my desire took hold of me, that would make me vibrate at a low frequency, since week after week I felt really bad by not winning the lottery.

Over the course, by being aware that I was going through a process of changes, I went through an instance of "self-analysis". I knew that I had to make an important decision that I am going to explain with these three options.

Option 1

I could dismiss everything I learned about the LoA and turn my lifestyle upside-down for fear that something like this would happen to me again. This means forgetting about meditations, readings oriented towards spiritual knowledge and growth, manifestation techniques and everything related to LoA, all of which already formed a part of my life.

This option meant going back to living just going through the motions, without wondering if there's something better waiting for me out there. Going back to the beliefs that the only way that leads to success is hard work after a struggle full of sacrifices. But for me that thought was out of date and not a viable option anymore.

Option 2

Be reckless about panic attacks and states of depression. Thinking that it was something that would never happen to me again, pretending about not seeing the problem and continuing with my life as I have been doing. This option required me to put all of my focus again entirely on the success of the lottery manifestation, with the help of the LoA.

I would go back to underestimating my health and once again direct my meditations specifically to the luxuries and the lifestyle that several million can provide. I could also add more combinations to my usual plays, to increase my confidence and to make myself believe that I would have a better chance at succeeding.

This alternative was not viable at all. If I chose it, I would ignore the sign that life, God or the Universe had put in front of me.

Option 3

Lastly, I saw it as feasible to take it as a necessary change that I had to undergo and use it in favor of my growth, of my personal evolution. I understood the situation as a test, a sign that God or the Universe had put in front of me to improve upon some aspect of me.

This meant going on with my life with the desire intact to achieve the lottery manifestation with the conscious use of the LoA. But this time, with the experience and the knowledge about the importance of health.

I needed to value my health through sports, good nutrition, meditations and all kinds of things that made me feel good.

Be grateful and aware of the privilege that having good health means. Just like being surrounded by affections such as the love of family, my girlfriend, my dog and my friends is a privilege I had to be thankful for.

Knowing that I don't control everything is more than okay. The lottery may or may not come, but my happiness would not depend on it because I would have other projects in mind that would occupy my time. These projects would motivate me to keep bringing happiness to my everyday life. Knowing that a good way to grow is to do it gradually and with clear goals is of great importance.

Without a doubt, I chose to continue my life with this last option.

As the days passed, the anxiety started to calm down until it was no longer a problem that hurt me and interfered with my main desire of winning the lottery. Once I learned my lesson, I was ready to implement new changes, to continue aligning myself in the frequency of my desire.

I don't hold any kind of grudge with myself, I no longer live that way, I learn from my mistakes, and I am grateful for the lesson they gave me. I don't blame myself thinking "how could I let this happen to me, what a fool I was".

I understood that it was part of a learning process, that it did nothing more than help me to be prepared for the manifestation of my desire.

The anxiety took me out of my comfort zone for a long time, but it also left me life lessons that will last forever inside of me. I channeled the episode with deep appreciation, away from blame, guilt, and victimization.

The power of detachment

Months later, I found myself playing the lottery regularly, but not like before, this time I did it without any pressure and with a real detachment of the results.

It didn't spark any kind of stress in me when I went to the agency to play, nor at the time of the draws did I feel strange, or in a weird way. What's more, on most occasions I forgot that it was a draw day, and I didn't even remember to check if my numbers had been drawn. This is how I welcomed the "letting go", I was allowing my desire to flow towards me. From then on, my days were different.

I could confirm firsthand the power of gratitude and of the phrase that goes like "when you feel well, you attract into your life good things".

Way back, I valued the apartment that I rented, the car that I drove and thus I opened the door to the car and the flat I wanted to buy. I was happy to live in a 538 square feet apartment, I saw all the positive things it had and that made me happy. It no longer seemed small and uncomfortable to me, it felt super cozy, easy to clean, easy to tidy up and I could pay for it every month without having to adjust my other expenses.

Something similar happened with my car, although it was not very old (around three years old) I looked at it and said to myself or to whoever was with me "woooow, my car is so nice", I enjoyed looking at it and driving it. As a result of this new way of living and feeling, I was making room for one of the spiritual laws that Deepak Chopra teaches us, THE LAW OF INTENT AND DESIRE.

This law talks about how recognizing the good we have is the basis of abundance. I stopped paying so much attention to what I could have in the future if my desire manifested itself and began to enjoy the here and now. My eyes were set on gazing at a prosperous future, but I no longer underestimated the present. That intention was the true power behind my wish because I was detached from the results.

My mindset was definitely transformed and now my way of thinking acknowledged that there was nothing wrong with having financial wealth. I thought it was extremely positive and if I happened to become a wealthy person, I knew how that situation would improve my life in every possible way. Always with my health issue on the back of my mind, without neglecting and valuing it. I knew now how to help myself, who to help and how to do it in the best way.

FINALLY, just 11 months after that summer night where I thought I was going crazy, I won the lottery without a doubt, thanks to the understanding and conscious use of the Law of Attraction.

The wonderful Law of Attraction works!

"If we don't learn to let go, if we don't do it, if the attachment is stronger than us and we stay there tied up, glued to those dreams, fantasies and illusions, the pain will grow without stopping and our sadness will be our road trip companion"

Jorge Bucay

Positive change

The day I decided to manifest the lottery, I didn't really appreciate my health. What changed during the course of this process is that what I used to think about health was turned on its head. It went from something that I didn't value or seemed like the most normal thing to have, to the fundamental aspect I'm thankful about every time I wake up and go to sleep. Not a single day goes without looking within me and feeling deeply grateful to be alive and healthy.

I am not saying that I am now an expert, not by any means, but in those beginnings as a practitioner of the LoA, because I didn't know how it operated, I ran into problems in my daily life, which I had never experienced before becoming aware of this law. This was due to the enormous expectations generated by trying the fulfillment of my wish and with the results not arriving.

I recommend that you never fall into despair, and you get to see what you want to manifest. Work hard within yourself and find situations that make you feel good in the present, this will raise your frequency to allow the arrival of what you expect.

The times of the Universe, God or whoever you believe in, are perfect. Don't let anxiety lead you to control them. If you have an unwanted or unpleasant experience, try to find the answer, surely it's a sign that, if understood, will give you wisdom so that you continue to evolve.

The winning combination: numerical synchronicity

"If you want to be successful, find someone who has

achieved the results you want and copy what they do and you'll achieve the same results".

Tony Robbins

It's clear that the key to winning the lottery is choosing the right numbers at the perfectly right time. Most of the time recurrent lottery players often make their decision based on significant dates such as birthdays or anniversaries. Some other frequent choices are to quickly write down numbers we have dreamt of, license numbers, numbers that appear to us daily, etc. Some scholars believe that the correct way is to choose certain numerical patterns that considerably increase the probabilities, even software has been created sold.

Regarding all that, the only thing I can tell you is that I have tried everything and absolutely nothing worked for me. What do I mean by this? Just that, I'm not saying it can't work for any random person, it's just that I have tried, but I didn't succeed that way.

When I became a regular lottery player, I used to choose a series of numbers that I liked, they were something like my "lucky" numbers. They had nothing to do with dates, ages from any of my family, license plates, or dreams. I never believed that luck would be on my side with that kind of choice. I believe that all of us have favorite or lucky numbers and my choice in the numbers that I would play frequently were along those lines.

I chose 6 numbers that I liked and I kept playing that ticket on a regular basis for more than a year, despite having already won once. Maybe you think I'm crazy to continue being a regular player if I have already won the jackpot once. But well... let me tell you something, I never mentioned that I won the lottery with the combination of numbers that I play frequently, although I do hope I will be able to do it one day, that's why I keep trying. After all, there is no rule that prevents someone from winning the jackpot more than once.

I firmly believe that winning the lottery depends on the vibrational frequency that one is in and not on chance. This book is about that, about how I managed to align my life with the desire to become a millionaire by playing the lottery. Having had the wonderful feeling of achieving it, I would love to repeat it. It's true that this time I do it from a more comfortable position and it's not my main desire, far from it. My head is focused on other types of short-, medium- and long-term goals.

Synchrodestiny

The way the winning numbers came to me was one that is usually quite successful among the different lotteries as I found out. The number combination was picked for me by a machine randomly.

It was an early Friday morning and for work related reasons I had gone to a city near where I live. While doing paperwork, I walked past a lottery agency and, as it was not a draw day, I decided that I would play later in my city.

Going out after drinking some coffee that same morning (still in that city), I saw another agency, but I didn't stop for the same reason either.

Having finished my work-related activities, we went for my car to return to my city. Minutes before taking the highway, the person who came with me asked me to stop to buy tobacco. When he got out of the car, I saw that there was another agency in front of where I stopped. This third opportunity, I changed my mind and decided to step down from the car to play 3 *random* ballots... one of them was the winner.

I decided to try out this style of playing, because I had become curious after passing and noticing so many agencies in such a short time. My gut told me to have the machine pick the numbers for me, after all there would be time to play my regular combinations.

If my anxiety had come out on top over me like so many other times, I would have played in the first agency I'd seen that day and the combination thrown by the machine would have been different from the winning ticket that I got a couple of hours later.

With everything that happened I can only conclude that the Universe or God decided to prove to me that, even if we sometimes find it difficult to understand, the situations we experience in our lives are necessary for us to be prepared to have our wish granted, and for it to come into fruition, you must show understanding and a certain degree of evolution. *Like I did that morning.*

I didn't let myself get carried away by my intense need of playing in the first place that I came across. Secondly, I noticed the signs (I had come to a stop in a place that was not usual for me) and thirdly, detaching myself from my regular numbers as my option.

The news

Nobody but me knew that I had played the lottery in another city, which was not a minor detail because that is how the "letting go" step was executed to perfection. I would not be listening to the news on the lookout for a winner from my city.

For the most part, I am not the person that checks numbers the day after the draw, because as I was saying, no matter how much I check them, I already knew that I didn't win. The news of a new millionaire in my city would have had such relevance that I would surely find out before going to sleep. Days later, I would check my tickets to see if I got any of the smaller prizes.

I'm going to tell you the story of how I found out I became a millionaire. Three days after the draw, while browsing through Twitter, I saw a tweet with a comment that said something along the lines of: "the one who doesn't care too much about the election of the new president is the winner of the National Lottery of... (Name of the city where the winning ballot had been played) ". When I glanced at the name of that city, I instantly remembered that I had played three tickets there where the numbers were picked at random. I hadn't even gotten a glimpse at the numbers the machine had given for me.

I visited a website that provides the information to see the numbers that were drawn and the amount the winner would receive. At that time I was not in my apartment, where I kept the tickets, which meant I could not check them, but I can assure you that just by looking at the name of the city and despite not having the faintest idea of what my numbers were, that I knew that the new millionaire was me. All that was left to do was to check to confirm and until that happened, I wouldn't tell a soul.

I headed out to the department with a mix of sensations. On the one hand, I was sure the winner was me; I had been working towards this goal with the LoA and life had shown me that there was no doubt that this wonderful law worked. I got into thinking about the whole process, the lessons I had obtained and the concrete possibility of having already achieved it. I would be lying if I said that from the moment I saw the tweet, until confirming my suspicions, that I hadn't felt fear or anxiety, it's the most logical thing in the world to have that feeling. But I can also guarantee that feelings of security and trust were also present in me.

I went into my apartment and as always, the first thing I did was to go out for a walk with my dog, I had never skipped over this step. He waits for this moment and I don't upset him.

Being at the park below the building, I began to take in all of nature, its energy and I internally asked it to help me be the winner. It may sound crazy to you, but I like to interact with plants and trees. I looked up at the sky and visualized myself going to the lottery to validate the ticket.

Going into the apartment again, I began to tremble. I went into my room to look for the tickets inside a box I had on top of the furniture next to the bed. I pulled out the tickets, turned on the computer, and went to the website to check the numbers.

When I saw that I was the winner, the tears began to fall down my face in large quantities. It had been so long since the last time. It was just me and my dog during this moment.

While he licked the tears of emotion that fell from my eyes, I was in a state of stillness. Hundreds of images came to mind, of all the moments I lived during the process. My happiness was immense, I had imagined this moment so many times, but when it actually happens, the emotion is difficult to put into words.

I knew that this was the closing of a very important phase in my life, probably the most crucial one. It's because of this desire that not only did I earn a few millions, but I also understood that I am here to be happy and the Law of Attraction will always be a tool available to carry out all the good things I want.

"Once you awaken you will never go back to sleep again and keep in mind that the hard moments happen when you find yourself in transition from one version of yourself to a better one"

Transition stage: flashback

Months after going through the experiences that increased my knowledge of love, health, and money, my desire to win the lottery by consciously using LoA remained as intact as my faith. With a different outlook on life, I was confident that I could become a millionaire with these means. For the most part, those of us who are introduced to spiritual teachings such as LoA have gone through extreme situations involving health, love

IGNACIO TORRES

or money, which introduced into our lives emotions charged with immense unhappiness. The
unfortunate events that we suffered during our
lives, serve to act as the catalyst that makes us
interested in trying out new "ways" (Law of Attraction), of teaching to help us change what makes us
feel unhappy.

The truth is that those of us who manage to
change those unwanted emotions and achieve
long-term success have to go through a transition
of ourselves into a new version. During this stage
of changes, it's logical that you go through rough
times, but only those of us who manage to gain the
learning and the strength from those experiences,
are the ones who advance to manifest our desires.

*I would like to highlight another part of that stage of
my life focused on manifesting the lottery.*

As I got more and more into studying the universal
laws, I started gradually moving away from what
up to that moment had been my life. My favorite hobbies used to be on Saturdays playing soccer
with friends and getting to hang out and chat for
hours with them and at night I liked to party with
my girlfriend or friends (depending on the occasion). During the week, on Wednesdays I would go
to dinner with a group of friends, on Thursdays
with some others and at least once a week I would
go to the movies with my girlfriend. On Sundays I
always had lunch with my family and usually the

night was spent with friends.

I used to be one of those big-time football fans. I loved going to the stadium to support my team and I didn't miss a single game. But all those interests that up until that moment were the greatest entertainment of my life changed. I started enjoying spending more time by myself, the only way I wanted to spend my free time was meditating, watching videos or reading books that would help to awaken my consciousness.

One day a friend texted me a YouTube video that talked about the phase I was going through (Dimension B, stages of spiritual awakening). That video that came into my life with great timing made me understand that, in order to align myself with the manifestation of my desire, I needed to pay attention to those aspects of my life that had made me so happy and that I later neglected. I needed to combine all the learnings obtained during this stage of my life, in order to be able for the lottery to manifest or rather, to allow my desire to flow towards me.

Little by little I returned to my weekly meals with friends, on Saturdays I never missed football again and I went back to going out with my girlfriend to parties and then the day arrived ...

The day of the manifestation

It was a Sunday, approximately 9.30am and my

dog was kissing my face to go for a walk and to relieve himself. I got up to go to the kitchen for a glass of water (I will delve into this question in part three) and took him outside. For many reasons this is one of those things that make my day start well, it's amazing to feel the happiness that an animal can transmit. He doesn't understand about good or bad days, he always wakes up happy and that pure love fills me with feelings of gratitude and happiness. Going out for a walk a few minutes after he wakes up is essential for him to relieve himself, but it also helps to take my day to the next level thanks to his positivity.

On Sundays, unlike weekdays, the traffic of both vehicles and people is almost non-existent, which means having a purer connection with nature. I can hear the sound of the birds, feel the weather (sun rays, rain, wind, etc.) smell the flowers, add to that the happiness that the company of my dog makes me feel. He knows that I will never fail him, that the first thing I'll do when I wake up is take him out for his walk, these actions fill me with positive vibes. Minutes after our walk, I go up to my apartment for breakfast, recharged with positive energies.

When I entered, I heard my girlfriend scream from the room, requesting a hug before breakfast. Obviously, I went to the bedroom more than happy to fulfill her request. After that beautiful moment, I went to prepare coffee with toast, while listening to relaxing music that helped me connect with my dreams, through visualizations.

While having breakfast, I watched videos from my cell phone, I don't remember well which ones, but I can tell you that they were either about the Law of Attraction or spiritual issues (I don't see any other type of content when I wake up) I don't occupy that part of the day with news, social media or anything that might take me away from my dreams and goals.

The rest of the day, I spent it mostly with my family. I went back to doing my normal routine from before. I enjoyed having lunch with my loved ones. That's why I went out to have lunch with my girlfriend, my daughter, my brothers, nephews and my dog at my father's house where we shared an extraordinary moment as a family. In my country it's a common tradition to have the whole family get together on Sundays and for this day the food of choice is usually centered around a type of roasted beef that we call "asado". I became a vegetarian a while back, so I ate a variety of different salads, while most of them ate meat.

After a long after-dinner, at around 3:00 PM I came back to my apartment. I took advantage of the free time I had to meditate and to continue connecting with my desires. On that day, with great emotion I imagined myself being healthy as I walked with my dog through the streets of Ocean Drive in

Miami Beach, and I felt the breeze of the wind near the beach while the sun rays hit my face in a very pleasant way.

I remember that meditation and I can't help but to get emotional as I write these words. The fact that I was able to fulfill a desire as strong as the one I had, knowing that I felt it strongly within me before manifesting it, learning about not letting the anxiety take over me (with the help of my faith) generates a great deal of pride for myself.

During the afternoon I had brunch with my girlfriend's family in a place in the city center, another great moment full of happiness. Finally, at night I returned to my apartment to have dinner with my friends and my girlfriend to finish the day alongside them watching a movie.

I had unknowingly become a millionaire that night, in the way I wanted it to happen after having worked for over a year. During the time of the draw, I never thought about the results from the lottery. Around that time, I was surely eating or already watching the movie (I don't remember well). The detachment towards my desire for several weeks had been taking place with total perfection.

I carried on with my life with the expectation that my manifestation would arrive, but without neglecting any aspect of my present. It came at the perfect time, those days I was a happy person, I was at a good place with my girlfriend, my family and my friends; in regard to health, the place that panic had occupied at some point through anxiety had ceased to exist, in its place now took their place things like good nutrition, exercise, gratitude and faith.

So far away was that summer Sunday and the days that followed where a spiritual crisis appeared in my life in the form of anxiety attacks, panic and depression. I'm thankful for having been able to overcome this stage of necessary learning because the uncertainty allowed me to get out of my comfort zone to continue my personal growth to manifest my desire.

When I prayed to God or the Universe, I always asked for economic abundance so that I could have the possibility of getting to know this wonderful planet in a comfortable way. Today I am gradually fulfilling that dream and thanks to these kinds of situations, each trip helped me gain a perspective of humility and solidarity that fills me with authentic happiness.

It's probable that, had I reached economic abundance in some other previous moment of my life, the feelings of arrogance, vanity and pride, would have taken control of my being and that I would have been unable to identify and correct the situation.

Thank you from the bottom of my heart

I am thankful for the day that I decided that I wanted something more for my life ...

I am thankful for that discomfort that led me to know the LoA ...

I am thankful for all the changes I had along the way ...

I am grateful for being able to express my wish ...

I am grateful for all the knowledge gained ...

I am thankful for my abundance ...

I am thankful for my health ...

... And above all I am deeply grateful because the Law of Attraction helped me to know myself and connect with my spiritual side, with my faith, which at some point I thought was lost.

I will never go through the motions again; I want and deserve the best ...

Thank you from the bottom of my heart.

"Let's start thinking about what we can be thankful for, and let us put our mind on that vibration, then let's observe the good that starts to come, because one thought leads to another thought"

Bob Proctor

SECOND PART

"Whatever the mind can conceive and believe, it can achieve"

Napoleon Hill

Introduction

When I came up with the idea of writing this book, I started to research the best way to approach it and I learned that there are two types of books: fiction and non-fiction. The former are just stories made up for entertaining purposes, and they may or may not teach something. The latter are books that always teach something and try to help improve an aspect of the reader's life.

I would love my story to help you in any way to improve any aspect of your life. I know that my wish to hit the jackpot isn't unique, I know there are a lot of people that would like the very same thing to happen in their lives. The privilege of having accomplished it made me think that it was my duty to tell my story the best I could, to help others that are passing through the same situation I was, before winning the lottery. Then you'll be able to win the lottery (or not), but that will depend on you, on the frequency in which you vibrate. However, you'll know that I did it, so it's possible: why can't you do it?

Use my precedent as inspiration, you know that at least one person could change their way of thinking and put the universal laws to work in their favor to manifest their dream, and that the dream was nothing but winning millions in the lottery. Consider that, in order to achieve it, they had to learn a lot in a period of a year and a half, and that's not a long period (believe me, it's not).

As I said in the beginning, my intention was not, and isn't, to sell you a magic formula. My real intention is that the experiences in my book teach you to improve some aspects of your life.

To stimulate hopes and emotions that help you connect with your desires, I prepared some questions for you. The first ones deal with the book itself, and the rest about you. They have the aim of helping you find what you want for your life. Many people think they know what they want, but they don't have the faintest idea. And that's the main reason why most people don't live the life they dream. They don't know exactly what they want because they didn't analyze what would happen in case their dream comes true. They don't feel it as real before it manifests, and the principal cause is that the majority lack faith. As a result, they don't have a plan of action that helps them achieve their goals, they see their objectives as impossible to accomplish.

It doesn't matter the amount of time you take to answer them. The valuable thing is that when you do, take the time to see inside you and get greater self-knowledge. By doing this, you'll detect your ideal way of life, and your mind will start working towards this new objective.

I would love you to share your answers with me. I will be delighted to read them. I can't help feeling grateful, taking part of my time to dedicate it to those that took theirs to read my story.

"The best way to overcome undesirable or negative thoughts and feelings is to cultivate the positive ones"

William Walker Atkinson

If you want to share your answers

with me, send them to thewonder-fullawofattraction@gmail.com

Questions

- According to your own experience, where would you locate this book, "fiction" or "non-fiction"?
- Can this book help you to improve any aspect of your life to achieve abundance?
- Do you think I only had luck? Do you think it was random? Or do you think that I manifested the lottery thanks to the conscious use of the LoA?
- What do you think made me have success with the manifestation of my desire?
- Have you gone through, or are you suffering any situation like mine (love, health or economy-related)?
- Do you think that I made a mistake somewhere?
- Is there something in which you don't agree with me?
- What do you want to manifest in your life? How do you plan to achieve it?
- What would you do if what you most want was already manifested?
- What have you done during the last year, month and week to progress in order to have the life you want?
- What do you think about money?
- Do you want to be a millionaire? Why? For what?
- Do you value your health? How?

- What would be your ideal relationship status?

- Do you believe in miracles? What would a miracle in your life be?
- How would the manifestation of your desire help others?
- What do you think about yourself?
- How are you feeling now? Do you think that you are vibrating in the right way to achieve what you want?
- What do you think your life is lacking in order to be abundant?
- Do you feel grateful? What about?
- What things you consider unimportant make you happy daily?

LOVE

If you have a relationship

- Do you have a relationship that leans towards evolution or conformity?
- Do you do things that you don't like, but you do them anyway with the purpose of not arguing with your partner? Do you think that this can be avoided?
- Are you afraid of being single? Why?

If you don't have a relationship

- Are you single because it's your desire?

- Do you think not having a partner is a problem?
- How do you think that your life will get better if you find someone special?
- Do you think that you can be happy being single?

"What is mutual is always the universal measurement to understand love. If two people want to coincide, there will always be time, willingness, interest and things will flow even if an enormous number of things get in the way. Love has no barriers, for everything else there's always an excuse. There it lies the difference between what comes to light up your life, and what comes to destroy you. (If it's not mutual, I don't want it)".

Andrés Alfonso

THIRD PART

<u>Techniques, tools and advice</u>

> **Keep your thoughts positive because your thoughts become your words. Keep your words positive because your words become your behavior. Keep your behavior positive because your behavior becomes your habits. Keep your habits positive because your habits become your values. Keep your values positive because your values become your destiny.**
>
> **Gandhi**

Even though none of these techniques were created by me, I put my personal touch in every single one, based on my experiences. But anyone who is familiarized with the LoA will recognize them and it's possible that you have already practiced some of them.

For those of you who have not, I invite you to incorporate some of these tools and pieces of advice in your daily life, as you find convenient. As everything, the key will be in the emotions that will emerge from your inside at the moment of doing something, because everything in life is trying to feel good.

These exercises are magnificent ways of helping us to manifest, this is because when we do them, we inject emotion into them. If you feel uncomfortable doing them, if you feel that it's not possible or that it's unreal, don't do them. If you do them without feeling like it, you'll be focusing on the absence of your desire, rather than the manifestation itself.

I have already said that I consider myself a good student rather than a teacher of the LoA. I don't think I know everything, but I incline towards the idea that stipulates that there's not a single method that suits every single human. A lot of people, when they want to obtain something, say: "it's impossible for me to achieve it", and time after that you can see that they've obtained their best possible result. This may be because their minds work the other way round: by internally saying these words, they generate emotion that may appear negative, but they aren't. The truth is that these statements are pretty effective for many people. This is because they have success with a particular behavior. Their 'negative' thought generates a reverse effect in their minds, and by expressing themselves in that way, it helps them achieve good results.

Therefore, we think that they are negative and pessimistic, but what they really emit is positivism and confidence. It's probable that many times they were successful that way, and they choose not to change their method.

Our thoughts are the protagonists of everything that has to do with us, because they are our point of attraction. Have you thought that those who say they are insecure are secure enough to state they are the opposite of what they say they are? Who didn't have classmates in school that always said they failed miserably, only to pass exams with merits? The subconscious doesn't have a unique way of working, so you need to understand the way you are working.

The period in my life in which I practiced these techniques with the purpose of becoming a millionaire led me to greater and better knowledge of myself. Until that moment, I just wanted to become a millionaire to stroke my ego, but after learning about the Law of Attraction and becoming a spiritual person, that changed.

Faith and spirituality paths, as the LoA is, give us something valuable that is difficult to find somewhere else, that is self-knowledge. In the path to manifest the lottery, I found myself and I recovered my faith as a spiritual person.

If you are looking for the same thing, be alert. Looking for economic abundance you may find yourself and your spiritual side.

If you take advantage of this self-knowledge, you'll gain a precious power, one that will take you to the realization of what you are looking for.

Take into account

If you are one of those who think that LoA exercises don't work, let me tell you something...

When you think that some of these techniques or tools don't work, it's because you are failing somewhere. These methods are real, and they have helped millions to achieve their dreams.

The most common mistake that makes you think that they aren't working the way you thought they would, is that you don't believe that your goal is achievable. Therefore, your emotions act according to that thought. First, you must think accordingly to what you want to achieve, and then take the proper measures that will give you what you really want.

The techniques help us to persevere with the emotions that emerge from our thoughts, that's the most important of these Law of Attraction tools. They are an effective way of aligning our thoughts with our desires, and in consequence they align us with the vibrational frequency we want to be in.

What we really want is freedom

A very useful tool to manifest our desires is to search inside us the true significance of what we want.

At first, I believed that what I wanted so much was to win the lottery just to be a millionaire, and at a certain point it was, but that statement was a half-truth. After much pondering over the possibility of my wish coming true, I realized that what I really wanted in my life was more freedom, in order to have more decision-making power.

Being economically abundant gives you the freedom to choose where to live (houses), how to move (cars, motorcycles), how to spend your free time (trips) or everything that money can buy. You are also free to choose who to help and how. The energy of money flowing is a great ally, but you should know how to manage it, and I don't mean only the financial part, but you must know what space you give to it in your daily life.

When I told you about the investments, I had made with the bank check from the jackpot, those also referred to health and love. I could have left money in fixed deposits and that, believe me, would have allowed me to live comfortably, but it was never an option. Instead, I preferred to do things that motivate me daily and keep me doing an activity that I like and that has a lot to do with health.

I also bet on love, because trusting in a business that my couple leads almost alone, allows us to continue growing and evolving together. It is a totally new aspect for us, and we manage it with mutual trust and the result is success.

The happiness that material things generate is true, but if we don't prepare ourselves, it can also be temporary, because what one feels when obtaining a good house or car is something really exciting, but over the course of time, perhaps it could become something habitual and what at first was a great euphoria, we mustn't let it become something "normal".

Two things are essential for this:

1- Always be grateful and aware of what you have. Gratitude, in addition to the daily freedom of being able to decide, is a feeling that brings constant happiness, and we shouldn't lose it or forget it.

2- When you become rich from one day to the next, you take off the enormous responsibility of worrying about money. You must use that as an advantage that helps you achieve happiness on a daily basis. Otherwise, it could become a problem.

The way I found that money is an ally of my happiness, is putting it into circulation in an activity that I like, that requires my effort, responsibility and that motivates me. In this way, the freedom I earned thanks to money is occupied with new projects that produce satisfaction daily.

That is why it is essential that you think, meditate

gacioORRES

and find out what you would really like to do in case of becoming a millionaire from one day to the other. Something that keeps your enthusiasm beyond the comforts and luxuries that money can give you.

Techniques and advice

Positive affirmations

One effective technique for me is to play nice music and write the affirmations feeling them as already manifested. But... What are affirmations and why is their use so popular with those who try to benefit daily from the LoA?

Affirmations are phrases we write, say and repeat so that our mind accepts them as real. The idea is that the mind believes that it is possible for this statement to manifest itself, using repetition and perseverance as the axis of the exercise.

The practice of the process will help us to awaken positive emotions. That's why it is essential that we feel good when doing it.

On the other hand, it is necessary that when we write our affirmations, keep in mind to always make them positive, in this way we are focusing on what we want and not on its absence. It is important to use everyday words that allow the statement to be understood in a simple way, eliminating any kind of comprehension problems. In this way, our mind assimilates the phrase perfectly.

A good way to make an affirmation is to replace a limiting belief that you know you have for another one that says the opposite in a positive way. For example:

"Thank you for having a wealth mentality"

"Thank you for so much self-love that helps me to be surrounded by people with affection and mutual respect"

"Every thought I make is creating the conditions for the future I wish"

"I am a healthy person and I allow myself to do all the activities I like"

"Everything is perfectly aligning for the arrival of my wishes"

"Thank you for this beautiful day"

"I am a healthy person and I enjoy that to the fullest"

"I deserve all the best"

When I started making my affirmations, I motivated myself by buying a green hardcover book. I chose that color because it is one that I love, and I link it to money. In short, it made me feel positive about that very important topic to me in those days.

Today I look at the book and I'm filled with happiness and pride, seeing that I could fulfill many of the desires I had set for myself by means of those affirmations. Of course, in order to achieve this, among other things, I learned that money isn't the only important thing. That is why I write weekly affirmations of gratitude goals that make me feel peace and joy.

"Thank you for being healthy", "Thank you for being surrounded by a lot of people that love me", "Thank you for giving me the opportunity to help many people", "Thanks for my mindset", "Day by day I meet the goals I set for myself", "My health is a privilege".

Desires... Tell them or not? To whom?

If we express our desire to someone that we feel that would help us raise our vibration by supporting us, it could be something positive. That person may make us feel good and one of the best ways to vibrate in tune with the source, is the feeling of happiness.

When I started this "winning the lottery with the Law of Attraction" thing, my intentions were highly positive, but one of the causes that made me not vibrate in tune with my desire was that practically every friend or relative I bumped into, I would tell them that I was going to win the lottery because I had learned how to do it with the use of the LoA. That statement on my part aroused ironic and risible responses, which generated feelings of mistrust in me. They made me believe I was being irrational, and I let myself be carried away by his words. Time showed me that in the end I was right, even though there are many lessons still to be learned. Among them, I learned that it would be best not to tell everyone about my plans. Sometimes it is more fruitful to work in silence, without sharing too much.

It isn't easy, but if you align yourself in tune with your desire, what you want will come to you perfectly, even better than you expected, don't let anyone else convince you otherwise, don't wear yourself out.

In my opinion, I recommend you not to tell people about your plans and wishes. If you want to share it with someone from your intimate circle who you think will always wish the best for you and will not question or judge you, you may do it, although it isn't my advice. Not everyone thinks as you do and even if they have the best intentions and they love you a lot, they might think differently and that's fine, there is nothing wrong with it. So, if you don't have absolute confidence in what they may think, just don't tell them. Look at your wish as an exclusive treasure and take action to see it manifested.

Visualize

Visualize big time that your dreams have already come true, emotions are ALWAYS the key.

Each day, take a moment to meditate, think, and visualize your dreams. The correct way to do it, according to LoA specialists, is using all the senses to bring wishes to life in our thoughts.

This is new to nobody because we have all used visualization. The difference is that now you do it consciously. Keys to the exercise: Infuse gratitude and happiness to your emotions so that the activity is pleasant.

It is important that you do it in detail and be constant, but with total detachment from results, so don't focus on the how and why, only think about the successful result.

You can visualize yourself feeling what you want, as I did with my apartment or my car. Touching the steering wheel, smelling the fragrance, feeling the breeze hitting my face as I rolled down the window, listening to the music that came from the speakers, etc. You can also visualize yourself in the third person, being an observer of yourself enjoying what you want to have.

You can do it with ambitious goals or simply when you wake up imagining your day with ideal results for the activities you have to do. The important thing is that during the experience you imagine your feelings at that moment. You need to feel happiness until you achieve a state of total gratitude and fulfillment.

You can set the place with aromas that you find pleasant such as candles, oils, incense, etc. A relaxing music or the sounds of nature may be helpful to add to the environment positive energies.

Let doubts go, have faith and trust that what you are asking for in your visualizations is already in the process of reaching you in a perfect way.

Finally, don't forget that this is just one more tool that the LoA has to help us manifest. This means that, if you add a plan of action to your visualizations, there are no limits to what God, or the Universe can deliver to you. Of course, you must believe that it is easy and possible.

The Universe's timing is perfect, even if it doesn't suit your ego

Dean Jackson

Visualization board

Put in a visible place in your home or work, a board with images cut out of magazines or printed from the computer, of everything that you would like to have. The house of your dreams, the car, landscapes of the places that you would like to visit, your family being happy, your health and everything that you want to reach that comes to your mind.

This tool is practical and allows you to be aware of what you want to manifest. It is a graphical representation that you'll see every single day that will help you generate emotions in line with your wishes, dreams or goals.

In my case I put it in the room, in front of my bed to see it when I wake up and when I go to bed.

A glass of water at night

Choose a musical frequency you think is harmonious or that helps you connect with your desires and let a glass of water rest with that sound during the night while you sleep.

You can leave it anywhere in the house, but the music you choose should last for the whole night.

The music that I choose is usually the same one that helps me to concentrate every time I do an "unguided" meditation. It can be "happiness frequencies 432hz", some sound of nature or just one that I like when searching on YouTube.

When you wake up the next day, go for that glass of water and drink it while you think about how your day will unfold. While you do it, put happy endings to every single action you are going to do during the day. That will make you start your day in a good mood and joy, from the very moment you wake up.

I like to feel that the water I drink in the first

moments after waking up is filled not only with fluid, but also with hours of harmonious music that brings with it good energies for the body and mind.

Lottery

A detail I consider very positive between the LoA and the lottery is when the intention of being a millionaire leads you to buy one or more lottery tickets. This action gives you the possibility that when you do manifestation exercises, do them with a real and pure feeling. That chance you generated when buying the ticket is telling your subconscious through the emotions that it should generate the illusion of being the winner, that there is a concrete possibility that you will be a millionaire very soon (the day of the next draw). You begin to move energies and visualize as if you already have everything the lottery millions can give you, in present time, not that you are going to have it after working hard for years.

That's a great way for your intention to connect positively with the materialization of your dreams and not with the absence of them. Intention, emotion and action.

Always put your attention on what you want to achieve and not on what you want to leave aside.

If you want to buy a new house, the car of your dreams, travel around the world or help relatives, but you don't have enough money, the lottery ticket you buy must help you in focusing your attention on all that you want to achieve. But not as distant possibilities, but a real and achievable one. That will make your emotions work positively, so that you can somehow fulfill those wishes.

Then, wealth can come to you in lots of different ways. Maybe it's not the lottery, but the Universe has a million ways to provide you with economic abundance. But that lottery ticket will have helped your emotions feel the possibility as real, showing a clear intention that you want to be a millionaire.

What started as an intention of becoming a millionaire can end giving you discipline and wisdom in many aspects, regardless of the lottery result.

The same way you take the decision that you want to be a millionaire, you must be honest with yourself and find the reason why you want that for your life. The answer will give you the ability to achieve it and the LoA will be the vehicle that leads you to that through the harmonization of your thoughts.

I always wanted to be a millionaire to live a life based on what my ego would have wanted, but of course, I didn't know. I was not awake; I was caught in a repetitive thought of what supposedly means being a millionaire. I had copied someone else's idea.

I thought that if one day I had a lot of money, I would spend my days partying, falling asleep in the morning and waking up at any time I want, without obeying anyone's orders. I would also have a fancy car to get the attention of the whole city, I'd be single with lots of different women or in a couple, but surely being unfaithful.

Well, the truth is that by aligning myself to the vibrational frequency of a jackpot, I turned out to learn to enjoy a very different life from the one I had in my mind for so long. And I am not at all saying that the other type of life is wrong or despicable, I learned not to judge people, I think it doesn't add up to nothing, but it's true that I found happiness with another lifestyle.

Don't do this!

When I came up with the idea of winning the lottery using the LoA, the first months I didn't manage to detach from my desire and consequently, I didn't allow it to flow towards me.

I was absolutely aware every Wednesday and Sunday of the draws. I saw them live on TV and the instant the first ball came out and didn't match my numbers, I would get furious saying that LoA was an invention.

What I was looking for was to be able to quickly manifest the lottery without effort, with no intention of aligning myself with the changes that the potential success would bring into my life. The only thing I did until then was to play some combination of numbers that would allow me to win. I'm not saying that no one can achieve it that way, in my case it wasn't like that. What changed the equation was realizing that I was making a huge mistake in my interpretation of the operation of the LoA. I understood that managing the times of the manifestation of my desire was something that was not up to me to determine. Never get in the way of that task because you are more likely to be able to express negative emotions like disappointment, anger and anxiety, and not your desire. Let God or the Universe do their part, they perfectly understand the how and why of everything, don't question them.

Never compromise your economy by playing. If a lottery ticket is worth 1 dollar and the top prizes range between 300,000 and 1,000,000 dollars, take it as such. By no means should you feel pressured to win the prize. Pick the numbers, play the amount and combinations that you think are convenient, but it shouldn't affect your economy in any way.

Usually there are two weekly draws, this would be 8 to 10 dollars per month and about $ 100 per year (approximately).

As I have already told you, I won with some random numbers, but you can win with the same combination or with your own way, it's a lie that there is a recipe.

If you win a minor prize or just feel inspired to invest a little more that week or month (as long as it doesn't affect your economy) you can do it. Maybe luck comes to you in a different way than the one you always thought it would.

The Law of Attraction usually gives us pleasant surprises that amaze us at its operation. When we start to see and analyze the pieces, we see how everything fits together and that we were the ones that made it happen.

Choose faith as an ally and open your mind so that emotions guide you to the answers you want to find. If you have doubts whether what you do is helping you to manifest your desires or not, ask the Universe, God or what you believe in for help, have faith and the answers will arrive. It is normal and positive to admit that you need help, a divine complement to guide you.

Make a list of the top five things you would do if you won the lottery. If you don't, and your life continues well in every aspect, it's a good sign. Never be a prisoner of a way of living, in that case, don't get attached to the results of the lottery prize. It is very probable that, to win the lottery using the LoA, good things begin to happen to your economy, independently of the result of the draw. This is because your thought patterns and actions will be inclined to your economic abundance.

I modified my list several times and when I managed to win the jackpot, I realized that this list improved my quality of life, but without it, I could go on living very happily.

Manage your ego

A well-managed ego helps you achieve your dreams. Many times, the ego makes you focus positively on big goals and that same ego can push you to achieve it. But be careful, it is more common for the ego to lead to personal dissatisfaction rather than success. That is why the role of humility is important in our lives, because it's humility that lets you know that you don't know everything, that you're not perfect and that this is normal (and that's ok).

It is logical that the ego works in conjunction with fear to keep us safe from hypothetical dangers that the changes could cause. Put to work in that cautious way, the ego keeps you within your zone of comfort and distances you from the manifestation of your dreams. But don't fear change if things don't go well in your life.

Humility is a factor that you should never lack in the desire for your manifestation, be it from the lottery, a partner or good health. Identify the ego feelings and humbly put them to work. For that it's going to be determining that you are humble with your actions and not only with your words.

Make the ego a great ally that is functional to your goals and never let it be your boss that tells you what to do. The key? MODESTY.

In my case, my ego made me believe that it was possible to be a millionaire by winning the lottery. At the beginning it was great because it opened doors to work on that goal, my ego generated the intention.

Then I made the mistake of letting my ego take over me, making me believe that if I achieved that manifestation, I could sweep the world away without having to consult anything or anyone about my actions. The absence of humility made me go through unwanted health worries, my ego let me know with anxiety, fear and depression that I hadn't been able to achieve my desire to win the lottery.

Don't try to interfere in the timing of your desire, otherwise you would be detrimental to the step of "letting go". It is logical that we generate expectations about the manifestation of what we want, but if you let anxiety become the dominant feeling, you will begin to live in the future without enjoying the present. This can lead to problems in your everyday life.

I spent several months living the two lottery days of every week with the expectation that my wish would be fulfilled that same day. As this wasn't happening, my anxiety led me to depression. That feeling made me go through unhappy moments that I had never felt before the LoA. Let the expectations of the fulfillment of your desire be the drivers for the realization of your aspirations, and nothing else. Act, persevere and recognize that you can't control everything.

Musical frequencies and the 55x5 technique

It doesn't matter what kind of frequency you hear, what affirmations you repeat or what meditation you do, the relevant thing is that at the time of any manifestation activity, you feel positive. If you notice that these actions help your well-being, you are on the right track, but if you feel that they are heavy or uncomfortable, they won't help you.

The more happiness you feel, the easier you shape the fulfillment of your wishes.

Thought patterns and intention, added to action, make the fulfillment of the order (or not).

An extraordinary combination of techniques is to write the affirmation of a wish but thanking as if it were already expressed and while you do it, you listen to a frequency that is pleasant to you. To this you can add the recognized 55x5 technique. This LoA tool consists in writing for 5 days, 55 times a statement about a desire that you wish to manifest.

The first step is that you already feel in a position to receive what you are going to affirm. Then find the time and a suitable place to write without being interrupted. So, there you can add the sound of a pleasant frequency or music to help you generate emotions in tune with your desire. Don't forget to do this exercise for 5 days, writing the affirmation 55 times each day.

Start with a simple wish. As you gain confidence you can do it with more important things.

In my case, I was able to fulfill all the wishes of my 55X5. The most important thing that gave rise to this book (lottery) happened only 9 months after having written it. If it doesn't arrive quickly, don't despair, remember that some wishes require a certain amount of time until you align with them, so that they reach you in the most perfect way.

I recommend you buy a notebook or book especially for this and write them with your own hand with a pen. This way you develop concentration for a long time and several days with what you want.

Music will help make that moment enjoyable, like a meditation technique, so the task will not become heavy. Remember that it is important to enjoy the process and if you feel that the exercise is tedious, it will be difficult for your emotions to produce thoughts in tune with what you write (your wishes).

Better than expected

I really believed that I could win the lottery, that's why I acted playing it every week, but to be honest, the thing I had least thought about was that I would win with some random numbers from an agency located in a city which isn't mine. In my visualizations I imagined the agent of the place I played regularly congratulating me on the award, shaking my hand and even uncorking a bottle of champagne. But the reality is that when I won, we hadn't even seen each other's face with the owner of the agency. For my convenience, I cashed the check directly at the lottery headquarters and for security I did it anonymously. The Universe made me get my wish in a way perfect, but everything was not exactly as expected, but better.

If it had happened the way I always imagined, everyone in my city would have found out who the winner was and that would have changed many things in my life that I didn't want, without a doubt.

Mental health

If thoughts are the key; half an hour before going to sleep, fill your mind with good thoughts, if you watch tv ... watch cheerful programs, if you read a book ... try it to give you knowledge that produces joy, if you listen to music ... it should help you connect with your dreams through your emotions.

You will see that little by little you will start dreaming of happy things and this will help to get up in good spirits to face the day.

Getting up always happy is important, use the first minutes of each day to remember your dreams. Then think about the day with all the activities that you are going to have and give them the best of the endings. Try to connect in a way that is within your reach with the energy of nature, you will surely be rewarded with its wonderful positivity.

Knowledge is power

If you read this book, you surely have an intention and a strong desire. And you are adding knowledge to that desire because no matter if it was of use or you think it was a waste of time, to do it you decided and the decisions we make always leave us something positive. So, when drawing conclusions from the book and its content, you gain experience and that gives you knowledge.

Now you must add some very important tools that we saw are essential for the LoA. Action is the main one, so don't sit still, act. Find the way you think is the most convenient, feed that desire and act until you achieve the expected results, commit yourself.

When you think of money and economic abundance

NEVER anchor yourself in the past, if you think you didn't have the best childhood, if you think that your past affected your present without you being the wrongdoer, or if you just stop to think about it, the only thing you are doing is closing the doors to abundance. Give yourself permission to live and feel that being a millionaire is totally possible.

Eliminate negative phrases regarding money, "I can't", "I don't have enough money", "That is something only rich people can do", "It's impossible". Also try to use the word "spend" as little as possible until it is permanently eradicated from your vocabulary and change it to "invest." Examples: if you are talking about holidays, mention that they aren't an expense, they are a healthy investment. If you go to a good restaurant, you don't spend much, you invest in yourself. And so on.

Read stories of millionaires, abundant or prosperous people you know. Learn to manage your money, train yourself the way you can in order to be ready when it comes to you.

Always be grateful for everything you have, focus on that and not on the absence of what you want and still don't have.

Faith and emotions

When you want to manifest, whether it's a cup of

coffee or the jackpot, what will tip the scales to achieve it is that you feel well in the process. Don't forget that the goal in any manifestation is happiness and the best bridge to lead us to it are emotions that make us feel good.

Have faith, the kind of faith to believe something as already manifested even if you can't see it yet.

Maintain your attitude in a way that makes you feel positive and a winner for as much time as you can. Positivity is a vibrational frequency that awakens well-being and consequently brings us happiness.

If you measure the lottery in probabilities, do it thinking that the better you feel, the more chances you have of winning it.

Never say: "When I win the lottery, I will be happy." Choose activities that help you daily, to vibrate high and give place to that magnificent manifestation. Study, understand and apply the art of allowing yourself things. You have to value all the good that surrounds you, feeling grateful to raise your vibrational frequency and achieve your desires. If you don't find happiness in your daily life, change what you feel is driving you away from happiness. I repeat, changes help us become happier, even if at first, they appear as insurmountable. Cheer up!

Thought becomes powerful when it prompts you

to act. A thought without any type of action hardly produces something, ever. If that thought causes you to move, you will end up doing something, which in most cases will lead to the achievement of your wishes.

<u>Mindset building</u>

To be happy is to stop being a victim of problems and become an author of our own story

Fernando Pessoa

Once before I won the lottery, I was chatting with a person from my intimate circle, she told me that she felt very sorry for the situation of one of her children. He couldn't find his way in life, and she didn't know how to help him.

The son was dissatisfied with the lifestyle the mother gave him, although she provided shelter, food and even paid for his studies. She mistakenly felt responsible for his constant state of unhappiness. The attempts to find a solution led to arguments and made the situation worse.

This happened and repeated over and over again because the conversations with his son were oriented to answers that never arrived. Those conversations were not an attempt to address a deep and definitive solution to the problem. The boy had low self-esteem, he needed to trust and believe in himself, but above all he needed to realize that his life depended on him and not on what others could give him.

Obviously, the mother had excellent intentions to help, she was the first that wanted to see him happy. But intentions may not be enough. Parents are a fundamental part of the construction of the mentality of our children but unfortunately it isn't uncommon that we don't promote a correct way of thinking, one that truly helps them in their lives.

At that time, I was still working for my father, it was some months before I became a millionaire, but my wealth mentality was already advanced, and that allowed me to think, speak and give advice as a rich person. Without realizing it, in many moments of the process, faith made me see myself as if my desire were already manifested.

Therefore, it was common for many acquaintances to come to me so that I could listen to them and give them my point of view on some issues. At that time, although my bank account still didn't show it, there was acquired knowledge that made me look like an abundant and prosperous person.

I told her that the best thing she could do was to clarify that she supported him in what he wants to do in his life. But that she should recede so that he could understand that his happiness depended on him and only on him. I told her to stop feeling guilty about past situations, because that was what his son assimilated, and it was very harmful to both of them.

This person's son was a young adolescent who, like many of us, blamed third persons for his own dissatisfaction. He didn't do well at studies or work. Every single project he stated was left half-finished. He had no direction, but he thought he was not responsible for the situation. I assumed that since he had a difficult childhood, it was not his fault that his life is unstable and unhappy.

His mother also felt guilty for the same reason. She thought that since her son hadn't enjoyed the best of childhoods, it affected him in such a way that he could not develop a happy life in the present and that was her fault.

Part of giving kids a good education, either as parents, teachers or any other role, is to help them build a strong wealth mentality from a young age, letting them know that they will be responsible for their lives.

They should be taught to set goals, never to underestimate the power of their will and their minds. Rich people never say they can't do it, they are always thinking about how to get what they want, eliminating guilt and blame of third persons.

The best advice you can pass on is what I did with this mother, and that is that well-being depends on you and that you can always choose, even in the most difficult moments, whether to let yourself sink or fight.

Time after I became a millionaire, this person reminded me of that conversation and told me that she had stopped coddling his son and that was partly thanks to that. He was gradually getting better; he was studying a degree with great interest and dedication. He had also gotten a job and consequently the relationship between them was better than ever.

When I refer to "before" or "after" I became a millionaire my intention is that you understand the importance of this way of thinking. When you have thoughts and knowledge of wealth, you are almost certainly going to live with that abundance (if you want), but you must make your subconscious understand and believe that this is the best way to achieve happiness.

This is how it happened to me, I thought like rich and felt like a millionaire before having the millions in my bank account. Wealth and poverty are also states and I assure you that only one of them brings us happiness. And the best way to start building a rich mentality is by taking responsibility for the situation you find yourself in, from that starting point you can advance to achieve your goals.

Learn to go through processes to manifest your desires. Keep in mind that you have to know how to benefit from the changes and reinvent yourself in order to enjoy the development of what you want to manifest. Wishes shouldn't awaken feelings of conflict. If they do, they will become something very difficult or impossible to do. Be constant and have faith. You must put expectations and illusion on your side. This way they will help to prevent anxiety, anguish and other unwanted feelings. Don't forget that a dream without a plan is only a wish in the air that can manifest itself, but it will be extremely difficult.

Be grateful for everything

If you aren't grateful for the little things in your present life, you won't be with the great things that the fulfillment of your wishes will bring.

By practicing the power of gratitude daily, you will generate a feeling of constant happiness and plenitude. The emotion generated by this state of gratification pushes you to meet the goals you set in a satisfactory way and not from the place of nonconformity.

Today

Live today as if it were the last day of your old life. Going to sleep thinking that the next day I was going to be a new millionaire generated emotions charged with happiness. The lottery twice a week allowed me to give more truth to those thoughts. I have no doubt that the repetition of that way of thinking made it become something real.

Direction is much more important than speed. If

you advance, even if it is step by step, you will always reach the desired destination, making mistakes is almost always moving forward. The important thing is to know where you want to go (objective) and how you want to achieve it (action).

Find your passion, give it a purpose, and build a habit.

Question your limiting beliefs

Question your limiting beliefs

Chofi TV - YouTube

Identify the limiting beliefs that prevent you from moving forward to achieve your goals. Then ask yourself if what you think is true. If it is, begin to doubt.

Find examples of that belief that demonstrate the opposite of what you think. Find people who are accurate examples that your belief isn't an absolute truth. If the thing you want is money, but you think rich people are evil, find examples that show they are not, because that belief is wrong and affects you if what you want to get is wealth.

Last but not least, write down a phrase that proves the opposite of your limiting belief: for example, "I always have money and I am a good person".

Have your own criteria

It is very good to learn from those who are in the place where we want to go. It is genuine to copy models, but it is also important that you develop your own criteria. When you hear something that seems interesting and you think it can help you in some aspect of your life, it is of extreme importance that you get information that motivates you to think, analyze and draw your own conclusions.

If I had permitted myself to be carried away by all the writers I read and the creators of the videos I watched, I would have stopped playing the lottery. Almost all of them agree that this game is something mediocre or that the Universe doesn't interfere directly with those issues. On the contrary, I chose to follow my strong desire to achieve success combining the wonderful LoA and the lottery. I didn't collapse in the difficult moments and overcame the obstacles that were presented to me. I didn't stop reading and learning about LoA, because almost every single author who writes about it recommends looking for economic abundance in other ways. Nonetheless, I persisted, found a balance and I implemented it. I kept reading, learning, making mistakes, but always moving forward because while I was operating in that way, I was aligning with my desire. Therefore, not only did I achieve my financial independence in a short time (lottery / wish), but I grew in all aspects of my life, to become a better person than I was before knowing the LoA.

I invite you to go and achieve whatever you want in your life. Commit to incorporating knowledge in any way you see useful, and then, in addition to being an observer, think and analyze to build your own criteria.

Through my own thinking, analysis and discrete actions, I became an abundant person, and in a way, everyone considers impossible or unreal. Do you think that is mediocre? Do you think the Universe or God doesn't intervene? I assure you that it is possible, that it isn't mediocre to try and that God or the Universe always find a way to guide you.

There is no single recipe for success, there are those who succeed through sacrifice, there are others who just try a little and get what they want and there is also a midpoint, where a mixture of the extremes gives the desired results.

The most important thing isn't to stay in a single position or thought. If you are trying a formula that you think doesn't lead to success, change it.

Don't expect different results always doing the same.

Letter to the past

A good way to leave behind all the bad things that happened to you and you feel that they don't allow you to move forward is to write a letter to your "me" from the past, making amends and expressing gratitude for the guidance.

The past can't be modified, it is something that

has already happened, so it's useless to think about "what could have happened if" because that way we are creating impossible alternatives. That would generate an unnecessary loss of energy.

On the contrary, if we accept the past, we are able to learn from it and that will give us an incredible advantage to develop ourselves in the present.

You can write the letter your own way, but you need to release all the emotions you feel at the moment of writing. It is essential to be honest, if you are angry, sad, disappointed or hurt, reflect it in your letter, because this time it's only going to be to say goodbye to all that.

I advise you to look for reasons to be thankful for. It's not important whether you had difficult situations or not. Without a doubt if you think you will find something you feel grateful for. It could be someone that made you feel good, someone who helped you, a song that gave you happiness, a pet or a place, but even in the worst moments there is something that makes us believe that everything is worth it.

Remember that the objective of this technique is to say goodbye to everything that doesn't allow you to progress or makes you feel bad in the present. Therefore, after writing the letter, it is necessary to burn it and give its ashes to the Universe.

This exercise is a great way to do a mental cleanse

of everything that you feel is anchoring you in the past, making you neglect the present. Break free!

Letter to money

Write a letter to money, I recommend that you start it asking for forgiveness. Surely if you think, you will find reasons to apologize for what you've thought about it. Don't make a god out of it, treat it like a normal person. Let it know that you need it and explain the reasons why you want it around. Tell it about those you would help if you had the possibility and thank money for having that possibility.

The objective of this exercise is to heal, to move the energies that you have in your subconscious and plant new beliefs. You can use it to let everything out, to leave behind a stage and start a new relationship with it.

Money is an energy and as such it shouldn't be compared in a bad way with people, it isn't one thing or the other. It is absolutely possible to own lots of money and be surrounded by affection. It's completely wrong that an energy (people) isn't compatible with another (money).

Finally, do what you want with the letter, do what makes you feel best. If you want, you can save it and read it when you consider necessary, you can also burn it, it doesn't matter. The most relevant thing is that you let everything out so that the new relationship you want with this energy is clear (money).

I am going to attach the letter that I wrote. It was one of the first tools that I used with LoA, and I keep it on my cell phone. It was handwritten and I decided to burn it and offer the ashes to the Universe, but it is something very personal. Oh, I almost forgot. After writing it, my relationship with that energy changed forever, because although it took about a year until the big day, after writing it I had an unusual flow of money. Yes, it's true, I was also using other tools so that economic abundance would reach me, but I consider this technique to be one of the most beautiful actions that I have ever done to begin aligning myself with my desire to win the lottery. When I wrote it, I felt strong and significant emotions, a change was starting in my life …

Dear money:

First of all, I would like to apologize, I consider that I was unfair to you. I thought those you were hanging out with were bad people, but I was wrong. I judged you and I did it in the worst way, almost without knowing you.

The truth is, I have never had the chance to relate to you in a good way and I would like that to change. I think you are a key that could open many doors that would make me happy. Having the possibility to be in contact with you in a fluid and frequent way, I could fulfill many wishes and help many people and animals.

With the help of your abundance, I would love to be able to travel around the world. Delving into the corners of paradise on this planet called Earth is one of my biggest dreams. If you are with me, I could do it in the best possible way and with those I love the most.

I would also like that together we give my family lots of things that I know would bring you happiness. But not only them, I have noticed that with you, I could help a lot of stray dogs. They need someone to take care of them.

I thank you because you allowed me to do many things that would have been impossible to achieve without you.

I hope this transition in the way I see you is a change that allows us to generate the greatest happi-

ness within our reach. With my intentions and your energy flowing, I have no doubt that we will achieve many important and happy things for many people and animals.

I say goodbye grateful, hoping that you arrive in abundance and stay forever in my life ...

Three ways to raise our vibrational frequency quickly and easily

Music

Music is an excellent tool we have if we want to raise our frequency without difficulty. With its sounds we can change our mood in just seconds. For those of us practitioners of LoA exercises, music is a great ally when we do activities because it helps us experience strong emotions that are those that connect with our conscious and unconscious thoughts.

When I managed to manifest the trip, one of the activities that made me desire it was that in addition to the sports event, a DJ I admire a lot would be performing in the same place. It seems unimportant, but it is not. When I was doing manifestation exercises to make the trip real, what helped me the most to generate positive emotions was the music of this DJ in combination with the visualizations of me seeing him live in that far-away country.

Because of the great emotion I included in the exercises, I was able to fulfill my wish to attend the show that evening. At times it looked impossible to accomplish, but there was something inside me that made me persist.

As it was a popular event, the tickets had been sold well in advance. So, when we arrived, we realized that accessing was going to be very difficult. The friends that I had gone with, seeing the difficulty to enter, chose to leave (they believed that they would waste their time if they stayed). It was true that the chances were minuscule: we didn't speak the language, we didn't know anyone on the site, and we didn't have a lot of money, but anyway I decided to stay and wait for the miracle.

After a half-hour period my friends had decided to leave, I began to talk with a person from my country that I had met minutes ago. The boy was in the same situation as me, he really wanted to enter, but didn't know how. At that moment I felt a strange sensation, even though I didn't lose hope, the minutes passed, and the situation got harder. More and more people arrived (with their tickets) and the nightclub didn't seem large enough to hold them all.

The "miracle" was about to happen. When the doors were almost closed due to lack of capacity, I saw a person coming out of the disco. He was a PR guy or something like that, he was undoubtedly someone important because the security employees followed their orders immediately. Then, he pointed to me and the Argentine boy next to me, as if allowing us to pass by jumping the queue. We looked in disbelief, the security man lifted the rope and we entered. I confess that I didn't even have the opportunity to thank the man who had that great gesture with us. He ordered, went back inside and I never saw him again.

Not only did I walk in and enjoy an evening as I had envisioned, but I was also able to take a picture with the DJ, I made new friends, but most importantly, that experience strengthened my belief in the power that the Law of Attraction leaves us at our disposal. What we can do through our positive emotions and thoughts is what we call miracles.

Connection with nature

This is an excellent way to recharge energy and change your frame of mind. It can be achieved by doing outdoor physical activity, meditating with the sounds of nature or by spending time with a loved one.

Nature is a great ally when it comes to eliminating stress and at the same time raising our vibrational frequencies. That is because our bodies need air and natural light, so when they receive these energies, it is normal that we feel better.

All of us have a neurobiological connection with nature, being in contact with it provides us with physical and mental well-being.

Find the way you think is the most pleasant and increase your frequency with the help of nature.

Meditation

This activity has multiple benefits. With the practice of meditation, we can relax and rest our minds, as well as eliminate any muscle rigidity.

This tool is a quick and easy way to raise our vibrations. With constant practice we achieve an internal connection that makes us aware of our body, our emotions and our thoughts, achieving a real state of well-being. If you don't feel in the best possible way, if your mind feels a bit chaotic, it is normal for these sensations to be reflected in the body, and there is no better way to change that state than by taking a moment to observe ourselves (meditation).

If you aren't a regular practitioner, you can start by trying 5 or 10 minutes, as you get more comfortable and then increase the number of minutes and the number of times you meditate.

There are many ways to meditate. I mainly use three of them:

YouTube guided meditations: I recommend that you find one that makes you feel comfortable in such a way that you enjoy that moment. It is important that you find extremely pleasant both the content of the words and the tone of voice.

Nature: meditating with the sound of nature is one of the ways in which we achieve an extremely pleasant connection. The one I enjoy most is the sea, but I also reach deep pleasant states in areas such as the mountains or simply in a park in my city.

432hz frequencies: it is said that if the music is tuned to that type of frequency, the balance of the sound of nature is achieved and generates profound effects on the consciousness and cells of our body. I simply prefer to emphasize that just by tuning it I can feel peace and harmony with ease.

There are many variants of this frequency in our cell phone apps (Apple Music, Spotify, YouTube, etc.) so that we can enjoy their beautiful sounds and connect emotions with positivity. Find the one that is most comfortable for you and try, you'll love it.

How to get the most out of the Law of Attraction

Once you start to increase and deepen your knowledge about the wonderful Law of Attraction, don't ask yourself what this law can do to improve your life, but how you can take advantage of its operation in order to improve your life.

Thinking, meditating and finding what you want is the first necessary action you must carry out. Try to be as specific as possible. Note that you can refine the details of your choice, but it is important that you define what you want, because it will make you truly enjoy what you asked for when it arrives. To choose, keep in mind that it isn't necessary to erase your past mistakes. In fact, if you do, you will eliminate the wisdom that the errors have given you.

When you choose, make sure that it isn't something ephemeral that gives you satisfaction sporadically. Ask big, with faith and enjoy the process. There is no one formula that tells us how long it may take for our wish to come true. In my case, little more than a year has passed since I asked to win the lottery, until I manifested it. Although I had my ups and downs, I consider that I enjoyed most of the process. Some learnings were difficult to overcome, it is true, but I also believe that each of them was totally necessary, because thanks to the lessons I learned, today I truly enjoy what I asked.

By the time the millions came to me, I was certain that I could be the winner at any time. My desire was intense, but with detachment from the results. Winning the lottery was not an urgent necessity for me. I was doing well in my job, but to think that I could be a millionaire through the lottery made me feel extremely positive emotions. I had neither attachment nor resistance. When I was meditating and I visualized myself as a grateful person for being the winner of the lottery, the anxiety to achieve it didn't exist.

That's why I always say that everything is about feeling good, if you want to manifest your desires, whatever they are, it is important that you feel good.

Find your passion, give it a purpose, and build a habit.

The signal of change

It is normal that sometimes we wonder if we are on the right road. To know how to interpret the signals, in addition to the emotions that are our fundamental axis, you can pay attention to other variables that will help you know if you are on the right track.

If over time you constantly feel you are stressed and your routine is no different to the average one, you need a change. As I mentioned in the book, the word "CHANGE" may sound ugly and unfriendly, but often only those who dare to make decisions that include important changes in their lives are the ones who end up achieving their dreams and living happily. So, if you feel you are way too stressed, that your body doesn't respond the way it should, it is a sign that you need a change.

When prayers are answered

For any prayer to be successful, do it by making positive affirmations. Believe that you have an infinite power capable of creating what you ask. Assume that you can generate what you affirm in your prayers, and no one will stop your wish from becoming reality. That is how it happened to me with the lottery.

My prayer:

"Thank you for giving me the possibility of having

economic abundance by means of the lottery. I know that this privilege is also a beautiful responsibility that I will use to generate a lot of happiness for me and others. I will make this energy be in constant circulation, creating the greatest benefit within my reach.

I also want to have the privilege of being able to convey thoughts of abundance, to help other people to eliminate all kinds of scarcity beliefs that they have in their subconscious.

God is the constant source of my economy and with him next to me, I satisfy all my needs.

I am deeply grateful because before achieving such a magnificent prize, the path to success gave me lessons that made me grow a lot as a person and being spiritual. I appreciate every teaching I had. "

Thank you, thank you, thank you.

The grateful mind is constantly fixed upon the best; therefore, it tends to become the best; it takes the form or character of the best and will receive the best.

Wallace D. Wattles

Made in the USA
Coppell, TX
28 January 2022